BLUE BOOK

THE DEFINITIVE GUIDE TO
WEDDING CORRESPONDENCE ETIQUETTE

CRANE & CO.

The Wedding Blue Book:
The Definitive Guide to Wedding Correspondence Etiquette

Editor: Amanda R. Haar
Design: Jen Rork Design

Expert Review and Consult:

   Baylor Stovall, wedding etiquette expert, Memphis, Tennessee

   Robert Hickey, Deputy Director, Protocol School of Washington®, Washington, D.C.

Published by Crane & Co., Inc.
30 South Street
Dalton, MA 01226

ISBN: 978-0-615-17896-7

Printed in the United States of America

This book is printed on acid-free paper.

Contents

A Note to the Happy Couple

Congratulations on your pending union. This is no doubt a very busy and exciting time filled with emotion and plenty of decision-making. The fact that you are reading this book means you are concerned with making sure every detail is attended to properly. We applaud you for that. And we also offer this bit of good news: the rules surrounding wedding stationery etiquette are no longer etched in stone. Today's couple has more room than ever to stretch and bend some long-standing rules to suit their particular circumstances.

As our society evolves, so does our etiquette. The fact that people are marrying later, the emergence of intercultural and interfaith marriages, second and third weddings, and alternative ceremonies are all contributing factors to the changing rules of etiquette. Many of the rules of etiquette were made (and continue to be made) to deal with changing social situations. Some of the etiquette deemed proper in this book would have been unthinkable generations ago. And, surely, a generation from now many of the guidelines presented here will seem archaic and obsolete.

Your Personalized WEDDING CHECKLIST

12 MONTHS PRIOR TO WEDDING   DATE_____
- O order save-the-date cards
- O order thank-you notes/stationery

11 MONTHS PRIOR TO WEDDING   DATE_____
- O mail save-the-date cards

4 TO 6 MONTHS PRIOR TO WEDDING   DATE_____
- O order wedding invitations
- O order direction and map cards
- O order transportation cards
- O order accommodation cards
- O order rehearsal dinner event invitations
- O order bridesmaids luncheon invitations
- O order day-after-wedding brunch event invitations

6 WEEKS PRIOR TO WEDDING   DATE_____
- O mail wedding invitations
- O mail direction and map cards
- O mail transportation cards
- O mail accommodation cards
- O mail rehearsal dinner invitations
- O mail bridesmaids luncheon invitations
- O mail day-after-wedding brunch event invitations
- O order wedding programs

- O order menu cards
- O order ceremony cards
- O order table cards and placecards
- O order favor cards
- O order announcements

WITHIN 2 WEEKS AFTER WEDDING   DATE_____
- O mail announcements
- O order correspondence cards/notes
- O order calling cards/gift enclosures
- O order at-home cards

When all is said and done, etiquette is based on common sense and courtesy. Your guests need certain information to get them to your wedding—the date, the time, and the location. You of course want to convey this as graciously as possible while injecting a bit of your own personality and a sense of the event into your wedding correspondence.

While this book will provide you with information on the basic etiquette surrounding wedding invitations and stationery, it is meant only as a guideline. As such, the information contained in these pages is meant to help direct, not dictate, how you choose to handle this most personal and important correspondence. Take what information you need to make your invitation work for you and don't worry about what you leave behind.

In the same way that no two couples, unions, or families are alike, no two invitation ensembles will ever be either. What's most important is that your invitation expresses your joy, invites your friends and loved ones to come celebrate, and marks the beginning of a new chapter in your life.

GETTING STARTED

As every couple comes to realize, staying organized while planning your wedding is all about keeping track of the details. In order to assist you in at least one area of this all-important effort, we've created a Wedding Checklist (left). This checklist will guide you in the choosing, ordering, and distributing of all the components of your wedding stationery ensemble.

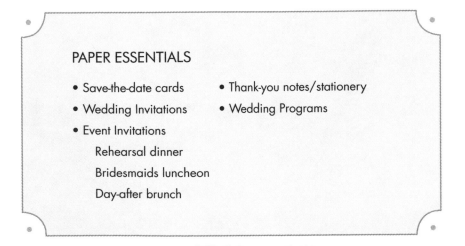

PAPER ESSENTIALS

- Save-the-date cards
- Wedding Invitations
- Event Invitations
    Rehearsal dinner
    Bridesmaids luncheon
    Day-after brunch
- Thank-you notes/stationery
- Wedding Programs

This includes not only your invitations, but the wedding program, table cards, menu cards, thank-you notes, and even your first set of personalized stationery as a part of a new couple.

By using this checklist, you'll ensure that you allow enough time to make a careful selection for each component and that you don't inadvertently leave any elements out.

Not all couples will choose to use all the components covered in the checklist. Again, there is no right or wrong to this task. Choose what works best for the type of ceremony you are having and for you as a couple. And by all means, have fun.

CHAPTER ONE

Before the Wedding

*S*tationery is an integral part of your entire wedding celebration. From the moment they open your save-the-date card to the day they receive your thank-you note, your guests will experience your wedding largely through the look and feel of your stationery. By choosing a theme and consistently expressing it through the quality of the paper, the color of the ink, a unique graphic element, or even a typestyle, you ensure that your wedding will be eagerly anticipated and remembered.

SAVE-THE-DATE CARDS

The first part of your wedding stationery is a save-the-date card. Sent at least three months before the wedding, these cards advise family and friends of your wedding plans and allow them to take your wedding date into consideration when making and scheduling their own vacation and travel plans.

If you are planning your wedding for a weekend during the holiday and summer seasons, a save-the-date card is essential to ensure your guests will be able to attend. Save-the-dates are also sent when a number of overseas

> *They met*
> OVER ICE CREAM IN CENTRAL PARK
>
> *He proposed*
> ON THE TOP OF THE EMPIRE STATE BUILDING (CORNY BUT TRUE)
>
> *Now*
> JEN & NICK ARE TYING THE KNOT
>
> *Please save August 23rd*
> FOR THEIR NEW YORK WEDDING, INVITATION TO FOLLOW

guests are invited or when a wedding is held in a resort area, since guests might like to plan a vacation around your wedding.

While it's nice to have your save-the-date cards match your invitation, it is not essential.

Save-the-dates often reflect the spirit of the entire wedding weekend or experience through unique designs and motifs. Palm trees, for example, might be used for a Floridian save-the-date or lobsters on one being sent for a wedding to be held in Maine. Many save-the-dates also include a printed photo of the happy couple-to-be.

To whom are save–the–date cards sent?

Save-the-date cards are often sent to all guests but it is especially important for out-of-town guests to receive them as they will have to make travel

UPDATED: *Invitation to Follow*

While save-the-date cards have been around for a while, it's still possible they may be mistaken for the actual invitation by some of your guests. For this reason, you should always include text at the bottom of the card noting "Invitation to follow." If you have a wedding website, you may want to include that address on the card as well.

arrangements. However, if they are sent only to your out-of-town guests and your out-of-town guests speak to your in-town guests, your in-town guests might feel slighted, thinking that they are not going to be invited to your wedding.

INVITATIONS TO AN ENGAGEMENT PARTY

An engagement is most often celebrated with a party hosted by the bride's parents. If the bride's parents live out of town it may be more practical for the groom's parents to host a party. The invitations should state that the event is being held in honor of the happy couple, although they do not usually mention that it is in honor of an engagement. Guests will undoubtedly figure it out on their own.

The invitations should reflect the type of party being given.

Mr. and Mrs. Andrew Jay Forrester

request the pleasure of your company

at a dinner in honor of

Miss Jennifer Marie Forrester

and

Mr. Nicholas Jude Strickland

Friday, the thirtieth of March

at seven o'clock

2830 Meadowbrook Drive

Bedford, New York

Our engagement will be announced at the party. How should the invitations read?

If your engagement is being announced at an engagement party, neither your name nor your fiancé's should appear on the invitation, as that would likely give away the surprise. The invitations read as though they are not for any special event other than to enjoy the company of family and good friends.

Two of my parents' closest friends have offered to host my engagement party. How should the invitations read?

When an engagement party is hosted by friends of your parents, the invitations are issued by your parents' friends so their names appear on the first line of the invitation or on the host line. Your parents' names are not mentioned.

INVITATIONS TO MEET YOU OR YOUR FIANCÉ

In lieu of an engagement party or in addition to an engagement party hosted by the other set of parents, a party to meet you or your fiancé may be in order. If, for example, your parents held an engagement party in New York and your fiancé's parents in California wanted to host a party as well, they may host a party "to meet" you. This party gives their family (your future in-laws) and friends an opportunity to get to know you before the wedding. The party is in your honor and the invitations allude to that.

To meet

Miss Jennifer Marie Forrester

Mr. and Mrs. John Peter Strickland

request the pleasure of your company

at a cocktail reception

etc.

INVITATIONS TO A BRIDAL SHOWER

The modern bridal shower is a throwback to the days when a bride brought her dowry to the marriage. Provided by her father, the dowry made her more attractive to potential husbands and gave the newly married couple material goods and finances to help them start their new lives together. Modern bridal showers, attended by family and friends, allow today's brides and grooms to have the basic necessities to furnish their new homes.

Bridal showers are traditionally hosted by one or more of the bride's friends. Bridesmaids who are not relatives of the bride are frequently hostesses. In the past it was considered inappropriate for a family member to host the event as it may have appeared they were soliciting gifts for the bride at the bride's request.

However, today it's not uncommon for the bride's sister, mother, or even aunt to give the shower. What's important is that the shower feels like a celebration of the pending union and not merely a gift-giving-and-gathering frenzy. Use your best judgment in determining what would be appropriate for your situation and circumstance.

Many bridal showers have gift themes, such as linens, kitchen, or lingerie. For older brides who already have a well-stocked home, kitchen, or boudoir, themes might include garden or travel. The invitation should reflect the type of shower being hosted and clearly state the theme if one is being used. Often a motif is incorporated to enhance the invitation and to reinforce the theme.

I'm being married for the second time. Is it appropriate for somebody to host a shower for me?

Historically, bridal showers have been reserved for first-time brides. But over the years tradition has changed and showers are now given for second-time brides, especially if she did not have one before her first wedding.

> **UPDATED:** *Couples Showers*
> Many couples are choosing to have "his and her" showers. Popular themes for these types of showers include "Stock the Bar" or "Kitchen and Tool Shed."

UPDATED: *Spa Parties and Other Luncheon Alternatives*

It's not uncommon for a bride to choose to treat her attendants to a day at the spa rather than host a sit-down lunch. The spa experience provides a more relaxed atmosphere for getting to know one another and for all to enjoy a pampering experience before the big day.

Other common alternatives to a traditional luncheon include makeovers, personal training sessions, manicures, and even group dance lessons or cooking classes.

opportunity to say a few private words of thanks to her attendants and to present them with gifts. Very often, jewelry or other accessories to be worn at the wedding are given.

Invitations to a bridesmaid event should be sent at least three weeks before the event. The nature of the event will guide the style of the invitation you use.

A Wedding Day Brunch or Luncheon

A Wedding Day Brunch or Luncheon is a nice way to make your out-of-town guests feel both comfortable and cared for. Traditionally hosted by a close friend of the bride's family, this event is held at the host's home for guests who have traveled from afar, close friends of the bride's family, and the members of the bridal party. The host traditionally sends the invitations, seeking guidance from the bride and her family on the specific names to be included on the guest list.

If yours is a destination wedding, you may want to give something that calls the setting to mind, such as a frame with palm trees. Alternatively, an item that can be used during the wedding trip, such as a snorkel and fins or a personalized ski scarf and hat, are also quite appropriate and thoughtful. Obviously, gifts of this nature would need to be given in advance of everyone's departure.

> **ROOTED IN TRADITION:** *Avoiding Bad Luck at the Brunch*
> In keeping with the tradition that the groom should not see the bride on the day of the wedding until the ceremony, many brides and grooms will stagger their appearances at the Wedding Day Brunch or Luncheon to avoid risking this bad luck omen.

REHEARSAL DINNER INVITATIONS

Custom suggests that the groom's parents host the rehearsal dinner and, therefore, issue its invitations. In circumstances where the groom's family is unable to host the event, the bride's family or a close relative or friend may hold one. Very often older couples or those marrying for a second time may choose to host the rehearsal dinner.

Regardless of who serves as host, the rehearsal dinner takes place on the night before the wedding and is given as a courtesy to the bride's family. Rehearsal dinner invitations are usually worded formally, but many times just first names are used. This less-formal style lets guests know how you, your fiancé, and your fiancé's parents wish to be addressed.

While an invitation to the rehearsal dinner should reflect the nature of the event, it should never compete with or upstage the wedding invitation.

Who is invited to the rehearsal dinner?

Traditionally, the rehearsal dinner was held for just the wedding party in order to get them fed after the rehearsal—and to give the bride's mother one less thing for which to be responsible. While many rehearsal dinners are still reserved for the wedding party, others have expanded to include thewedding party, their spouses or dates, and out-of-town guests.

When are rehearsal dinner invitations sent?

The invitations are sent two weeks before the wedding. By mailing them well after the wedding invitation has been sent, you are assured that you will not upstage the primary invitation.

Mr. and Mrs. John Peter Strickland

request the pleasure of your company

at the rehearsal dinner

in honour of

Miss Jennifer Marie Forrester

and

Mr. Nicholas Jude Strickland

Friday, the twenty-second of August

at half after seven o'clock

Tappan Hill

Tarrytown, New York

Nellie and John Strickland

request the pleasure of your company

at the rehearsal dinner for

jen & nick

Friday, August 22nd

at 7:30pm

Tappan Hill

Tarrytown, New York

▲ Sample rehearsal dinner invitations

ROOTED IN TRADITION: *Fill-In Invitations*

For small rehearsal dinners it is still considered appropriate for the groom's parents to extend invitations through a handwritten note on their "Mr. and Mrs." folded notes or a fill-in invitation.

Very few people are being invited to our rehearsal dinner. Do we need engraved invitations?

Traditional, engraved invitations are rarely used for rehearsal dinners any more. There are other printing options, such as thermography, that produce an attractive, formal invitation at a much more reasonable cost.

PRE-WEDDING THANK-YOU NOTES

A bride may begin to receive gifts from close friends and family or to be honored at an engagement party very soon after the engagement. It is essential to have stationery on hand to be able to promptly send a note of thanks. If you do not have personalized stationery at the time of your engagement, make a plan to visit a stationer and place an order. Because receipt of your notes will take a while, you may want to pick up a set of notes with the initial of your maiden last name already printed on it. These will hold you over until your personalized notes arrive.

Traditionally, a bride's thank you was an ecru fold-over with her maiden monogram blind-embossed on the front. This type of elegant and formal note is still relevant for today's bride, but there are many choices of colors and

UPDATED: *Something for Every Occasion*

Many modern brides prefer to have a few different styles of notes on hand during her engagement. Thank-you notes to a close friend or for a fun shower gift may be more casual and spirited than a note you might send to a great-aunt for a set of crystal champagne flutes.

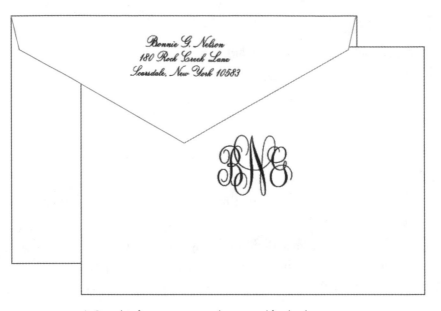

Bonnie G. Nelson
180 Rock Creek Lane
Scarsdale, New York 10583

▲ Sample of a monogrammed note used for thank-you notes

monogram styles that can be customized to best reflect the bride's personality while still adhering to tradition.

May I use a flat card to write my thank-you notes?

The most important thing about your correspondence is the sincerity of the note and the promptness with which it is sent. Flat cards and other nontraditional papers and notes that express your personality and are in keeping with the tone of the thank you can certainly be used. Some couples choose to have personalized flat cards with just their first names. These cards can be used throughout the entire wedding process and beyond. It is also appropriate for the groom to pen thank-you notes on his own stationery for gifts received at a his-and-her shower or other gestures of kindness that benefited you both before the wedding.

CHAPTER TWO

Wedding Invitations & Announcements

*W*hile save-the-date cards provide an initial glimpse of the spirit and theme of your wedding, your invitation and all the other stationery elements that precede the ceremony truly set the stage. You have many options in terms of tone, style, and overall formality or informality. Every element, from the paper stock and the wording, to the components of your invitation and the ink color speaks volumes about your affair. The best guidance one can offer a couple is to be thoughtful and consistent with your selections. A carefully selected and planned invitation set will honor the event as well as those you have chosen to be a part of it.

SELECTING YOUR WEDDING INVITATION

Wedding invitations set the tone for the wedding. If you haven't sent a save-the-date card, the invitation is the first exposure people will have to your wedding, and will shape your guests' first impressions. Not only do your invitations tell them where and when your wedding is being held, they subtly tell them through style, paper choice, and wording how formal it is and how they should dress.

ROOTED IN TRADITION: *What is a Traditional Invitation?*
Traditionally, wedding invitations were engraved on a white or ecru rectangular piece of stationery that featured an embossed border or frame. Traditional invitation sets tended to use one of several specific typefaces (see page 31) and always include an inner envelope containing the invitation, a reception card, a reply card, an overlay tissue, and a stamped, preprinted reply envelope, all sent inside an outer envelope.

When you select your wedding invitations, keep in mind what kind of wedding you are having. Your invitations and your wedding should complement one another. While formal invitations are appropriate for, among other things, a traditional church wedding, something less formal and more colorful may be a better choice for a wedding held at sunset on a beach.

Wedding invitations should be ordered at least three months before your wedding. This should leave you enough time for producing your invitations and addressing and mailing them. (Wedding invitations should be mailed four to six weeks before the wedding.) Of course, it is best to order them as soon as you have all the necessary information.

Where should I purchase my wedding invitations?

Many places sell wedding invitations including stationery stores, engravers, department stores, and specialty or online stores. When selecting a stationer, you should look for one who has expertise in selling wedding invitations and with whom you feel comfortable working. A quality stationer will be a valuable resource and not just an order taker. Your stationer should be able to understand and interpret your vision for your invitation and offer ideas and guidance on its design. They should be able to answer or find the answer to any questions regarding types of printing, paper stock, the components of your invitation and wedding set, and timing for mailing. They should also be able to address issues of etiquette and wording for your invitation.

If after a first meeting you're not comfortable with a stationer's competencies in these areas, keep looking. You don't want to risk disappointment on any element of your wedding stationery.

ROOTED IN TRADITION: *Earth-Friendly and Everlasting*

Concern for the environment is becoming increasingly important among today's consumers. One's choice of paper for stationery, invitations, and announcements is no exception.

Crane's 100% cotton papers are ideal for those looking for an environmentally responsible paper that doesn't sacrifice quality. Not a single tree falls to make Crane's 100% cotton paper, but rather cotton fibers recovered from the cotton-ginning and cottonseed-oil industries—fibers that otherwise would be discarded—are used. Crane papers are elegant and earth-friendly.

Cotton fibers are inherently white and are almost pure cellulose. They require fewer chemicals and produce less waste than other raw materials for papermaking. And, as a result, letters, invitations, and announcements on Crane paper will retain their beauty for generations to come.

Choosing a Paper for Your Wedding Invitation

Your wedding papers will most likely be made from either cotton or wood. The first true papers were made from cotton almost two thousand years ago. Wood-pulp papers came into being in the 1800s during the industrial revolution. They supplanted cotton-fiber papers for many uses because of their lower cost and the seemingly endless supply of trees.

Cotton papers are the ideal choice for invitations that are to be engraved or letterpressed. Because cotton fibers are soft and strong, they fully absorb and accept the deep impressions created through these printing processes. The inherent elegance and artistic qualities of both printing methods are truly best displayed and appreciated on 100% cotton paper.

Choosing a Format for Your Wedding Invitation

A well-chosen wedding invitation reflects the character of the individuals being joined and the nature of the ceremony planned. In much the same way that no couple is alike, no two wedding invitations need ever be alike either. Today brides and grooms have a virtually limitless selection of formats to choose from and can even create their own. While traditional styles are typically more formal and are always appropriate, those same styles can be easily updated to express your values while offering up a touch of personality.

The most traditional invitation format has a fold on the left-hand side and opens like a book. This type of stationery is called a wedding sheet. The invitation may be either plain or paneled. Paneled invitations have a blind-embossed frame. The decision on which one to choose is usually determined by the lettering style selected.

Another traditional-style invitation is a heavyweight flat card. It can be as simple as an ecru or white card, to those incorporating a panel, hand bordering, or beveled edges with hand-applied gold or silver leaf. It's also not uncommon to see couples add their own flair to this traditional style by using a colored stock with a colored ink and even embellishing it with a somewhat casual motif.

No matter which format you choose, you should always ask to see a proof so you can see what the invitation will look like before it goes to press. While some script lettering styles can look beautiful on a sample invitation, they may need to be condensed or expanded to fit the format of your invitation and consequently not look the way you anticipated. A proof eliminates surprises and is a small, wise investment.

What size should my invitation be?

While in the past there were traditional sizes for invitations, today's couples are bound only by their imagination when choosing a size for their invitation. When designing your invitation, make sure there is an appropriate-sized envelope for the invitation and all the components. You should also be aware that any over- or off-sized invitations may require extra postage.

Mr. and Mrs. David Leyton Jones

request the honour of your presence

at the marriage of their daughter

Bronwyn Alice

to

Mr. Andrew Philip Smallwood

Saturday, the fifth of June

two thousand ten

at half after eleven o'clock

Brandywine Valley Baptist Church

Wilmington, Delaware

DR. AND MRS. SAM NAUGHTON

REQUEST THE HONOR OF YOUR COMPANY

AT THE MARRIAGE OF THEIR DAUGHTER

Kelly Ann

TO

Michael Plimpton

SATURDAY, THE THIRTEENTH OF JUNE

TWO THOUSAND TEN

FOUR O'CLOCK IN THE AFTERNOON

WAVE HILL

BRONX, NEW YORK

Reception Immediately following

▲ Sample wedding invitations

LEEZA
FARELLA

OTTAVIO
GIANNINI

together with their families
request the pleasure of your company
at their wedding and celebration
Saturday, the eighth of May
Two thousand ten
at six o'clock in the evening

56 Kensington Parkway
Kansas City, Missouri

Designing Your Invitation

What color paper should I use?

Formal wedding invitations are traditionally engraved on either ecru or white stationery. Ecru is the color you may know as buff, cream, ivory, or eggshell. It is the off-white color that is typically associated with wedding invitations. Ecru is the more popular traditional choice in the Americas while white is the color of choice in Europe.

However, invitations can be produced on literally any color paper. In fact it's quite common for a couple to choose an invitation that reflects the overall color scheme of their wedding. The color that you choose is first and foremost a matter of personal preference.

There must be hundreds of different lettering styles. How do I go about choosing one?

Selecting a lettering style can be a challenging and confusing task. While helpful, style charts present just one line of each particular style surrounded by a myriad of other styles. They do not give you a very good idea of how the whole invitation will look. One of the best ways to choose a lettering style is to look at sample invitations. Your stationer should have an ample supply for you to review. This allows you to see what your invitations will look like in each lettering style. Be sure to focus on how the specific letters appear, especially those in your name. With some script typefaces, a capital "S" may look more like a "J." A letter-by-letter review will help you avoid any unwanted surprises.

But whether your invitation is traditional or not, the lettering style you choose should reflect the tone of your wedding and your personal taste.

What color ink should I use?

While black ink remains the most formal and popular ink color, there really are no hard and fast rules when it comes to the color of ink on your invitation. Your own personal design aesthetic and legibility should guide you in your selection.

Many couples choose a color that reflects the season or tone of the event or one that coordinates with the color palette of the wedding.

A SAMPLING
OF WEDDING TYPESTYLES

mr. and mrs. andrew jay forrester
ASHLYN

Mr. and Mrs. Andrew Jay Forrester
BASKERVILLE ROMAN ITALIC

Mr. and Mrs. Andrew Jay Forrester
BERNHARD FASHION

Mr. and Mrs. Andrew Jay Forrester
BICKHAM SCRIPT

MR. AND MRS. ANDREW JAY FORRESTER
CENTAUR

MR. AND MRS. ANDREW JAY FORRESTER
COPPERPLATE

Mr. and Mrs. Andrew Jay Forrester
FINEHAND

MR. AND MRS. ANDREW JAY FORRESTER
HANNA

Mr. and Mrs. Andrew Jay Forrester
STATESMAN

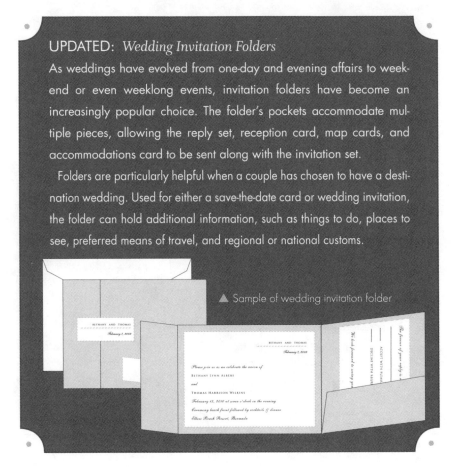

UPDATED: *Wedding Invitation Folders*

As weddings have evolved from one-day and evening affairs to weekend or even weeklong events, invitation folders have become an increasingly popular choice. The folder's pockets accommodate multiple pieces, allowing the reply set, reception card, map cards, and accommodations card to be sent along with the invitation set.

Folders are particularly helpful when a couple has chosen to have a destination wedding. Used for either a save-the-date card or wedding invitation, the folder can hold additional information, such as things to do, places to see, preferred means of travel, and regional or national customs.

▲ Sample of wedding invitation folder

The printing process, as well as the color of the paper you choose, will also impact your ink color selection. For example, an engraved metallic monogram or motif will have a jewel-like quality to it that cannot be matched by any other printing process. To avoid any unwelcome surprises, ask your stationer to provide you examples of your ink and paper choice produced with the method you will be using for your invitation.

What is engraving?

Engraving is one of the oldest and most beautiful processes for reproducing images on paper. It was developed during the 1500s and was initially used to reproduce the documents and announcements that were at that time copied by hand. The appeal of engraving is in the exquisite detail created by its three-dimensional impression.

Engravers were talented craftsmen who carried their trade from the Old World to the Americas. Their craft was not only used to produce stationery and announcements but also currency papers, such as stocks, bonds, and dollar bills. Two of the United States' most famous engravers were Paul Revere and Benjamin Franklin.

The most elegant invitations are still engraved. It has a warmth and elegance all its own that conveys an unspoken message of distinction and timelessness. The first step in creating such a truly unique invitation is the transference of the image, or text, to a copper plate. The invitation copy is etched in reverse into a copper plate. Ink is deposited into the resulting cavity. The engraving press then forces the paper into the cavity, creating a raised impression. The paper is literally raised with the ink adhering to its surface. This is the process that creates the sharp definition that is associated with the engraving art.

Every engraved invitation is fed into the engraving press by hand. The press is adjusted to accommodate the specific typestyle, paper, and type selected by the customer. For certain types of metallic inks, an additional pass through the engraving press is required to "burnish" the image and to bring out the richness of the ink's tone. Because there is no mass production in engraving, each impression, each invitation, is a customized one. The tangible elegance and quality of each piece instantly communicates a commitment to quality, down to the last detail.

How can I tell if an invitation is engraved?

The easiest way is to turn it over and look at the back. If there is an indentation, it is engraved.

The indentation is caused by the pressure the engraving press exerts on the paper when it forces the paper into the cavity of the die. No other process produces an indentation. When you look at the front of the indentation, you will notice its "bruise." The invitation will have a gentle wave or ripple to it, giving it a look of distinction. Run your fingers across it. You will feel the softness of the cotton paper interrupted by the sharp, crisp lines that can be created only by engraving.

In addition, the lettering on an engraved invitation will have a flat, matte finish as opposed to the glossy or shiny appearance typically associated with other types of printing, such as thermography.

What is blind–embossing?

Blind-embossing (or just "embossing") is a process similar to engraving. As with engraving, a raised impression is created from a copper plate. Unlike engraving, no ink is used. Blind-embossing is commonly used for a family coat of arms, the return address on the outside envelopes, and monogrammed thank-you notes. Dies made for blind-embossing can be used again to blind-emboss. They cannot, however, be used for engraving with ink.

What is letterpress?

Letterpress began in Europe in the 14th century as an alternative to laborious calligraphy. Type was handcast and individual characters were hand-set into lines until machine-set composition made the process easier. Today, many designers are returning to the craft of letterpress as a unique option to other printing methods.

Often used in combination with soft, handmade papers, the raised printing surfaces on a letterpress plate leave a deep impression on the paper. The depth of the image is accentuated by the ink and minute shadows created within the impression. Letterpress offers a warmth and quality that is not easily duplicated by other printing methods.

What is thermography?

Thermography is sometimes called "raised printing." Unlike engraving where the paper is actually raised, the raise in thermography is created by a resinous powder that is melted over the flat-printed ink. Thermography is less expensive than engraving and can give your invitations a look similar to but not quite as nice as engraving. The letters on a thermographed invitation will have a shiny appearance.

What is lithography?

Also referred to as flat or offset printing, lithography uses ink to print lettering or images onto paper. Lithography is the printing process most commonly used for mass-produced items such as posters, books, and newspapers. The finished product has a flat finish as opposed to the raised or indented finishes of engraved or letterpressed items. Lithography is the most affordable printing option.

A Look Back: PERSONALIZED INVITATIONS

The most formal wedding invitations of the past were personalized. Personalized invitations were not only elegant, but they honored guests by including their name on the invitation. Names were handwritten in black ink in a reserved space on the invitations and in a handwriting style that matched the address on the envelopes. Very often, a calligrapher was retained for the task.

Mr. and Mrs. Andrew Jay Forrester

request the honour of the presence of

Mr. & Mrs. Glen Rougeau

at the marriage of their daughter

Jennifer Marie

to

COMPOSING YOUR WEDDING INVITATION

The traditional wedding invitation has changed little over the years. Its essential purpose is to invite your guests and to tell them where and when your wedding is being held. It is that simplicity, coupled with fine paper and handsome design, that makes formal wedding invitations so elegant.

There are a number of basic points of etiquette that should be followed when wording a traditional wedding invitation. The following section covers the correct wording line by line and touches on other elements that a couple may choose to include on their invitation.

Mr. and Mrs. Andrew Jay Forrester — host line

request the honour of your presence

at the marriage of their daughter — request lines

Jennifer Marie — bride's name

to — joining word

Mr. Nicholas Jude Strickland — groom's name

Saturday, the twenty-first of August — date line

Two thousand and ten — year line

at six o'clock — time line

Church of Christ — location

1223 Roaring Brook Road — address

Bedford, New York — city and state

Host Line

Wedding invitations are properly issued by the parents of the bride. This tradition and the tradition of the bride's father giving away the bride have their origins in the days when the bride's father made the marriage arrangements for his daughter by negotiating the size of her dowry. Today, the traditions continue with the bride's family customarily hosting the wedding. Assuming the bride's parents are still married, their names appear on the first line of the wedding invitations.

If the bride's parents are divorced, the parents' names appear on separate lines with the mother's name always appearing first. The word "and" is not used to join them.

For more information on handling the wording of invitations involving *Divorced Parents*, see page 43.

Mr. and Mrs. Andrew Jay Forrester

request the honour of your presence

at the marriage of their daughter

Jennifer Marie

etc.

One of my parents is a medical doctor and the other is not. How is that worded?

Medical doctors do use their professional titles. "Doctor" should be written out. However, it may be abbreviated to "Dr." if your parent's name is exceptionally long.

The parent who is a doctor is listed first on the invitation. The other parent's title and name, preceded by "and," appears on the second line. The use of "and" indicates that they are married. Were you not to use "and" it would appear as though your parents were divorced.

Dear Aunt Meg and Uncle Steven,

Nicholas and I will be getting married on Saturday, August twenty third at six o'clock at the Church of Christ in Bedford. The reception will be held afterwards at the club.

We want you to be a part of our wedding.

Love,
Jennifer

A Look Back: HANDWRITTEN INVITATIONS

In the past, invitations for very small weddings involving only close friends and immediate family were handwritten. Invitations took the form of a short note inviting guests to the wedding. The wording varied, depending on the closeness to the guest. An invitation to someone close to the couple was written in a more familiar tone while a more standard wedding format was used for more distant relatives and other guests not so well acquainted with the couple.

Handwritten invitations were traditionally written in black ink on plain, ecru, or white letter sheets. (Letter sheets are sheets of stationery that have a fold on the left-hand side. They fold a second time from top to bottom to fit a single envelope.)

Doctor Mary Chance Forrester

and Mr. Andrew Jay Forrester

request the honour of your presence

at the marriage of their daughter

etc.

Both of my parents are medical doctors. How do their names read?

Your parents' names may read "The Doctors Forrester," "Doctor Andrew Jay Forrester/ and Doctor Mary Chance Forrester," or as "Doctor and Mrs. Andrew Jay Forrester."

My mother kept her maiden name. How should my parents' names read?

Your mother's name should appear on the first line of the invitation and your father's name, preceded by "and," on the second. Either the titles of "Ms." and "Mr." or no titles are used in this format.

Mary Ellen Chance

and Andrew Jay Forrester

request the honour of your presence

at the marriage of their daughter

etc.

ROOTED IN TRADITION: *The Coat of Arms*

Some of the most distinctive and traditional wedding invitations feature a coat of arms.

Originally, a coat of arms was the armor a knight wore into battle. To identify him as a friend or foe, an insignia was emblazed on the front. This insignia was transformed into what we now think of as a coat of arms: a small symbol, unique to each family.

A full coat of arms is made up of the crest, the helmet, the shield, and the motto. Mantling, a representation of the cloth worn by a knight that protected the back of the head and neck, may also be added. The coat of arms "belongs" to the men in the family and may be used on invitations issued by a man or by a man and his wife. Since, historically, women did not go into battle, they do not use a full coat of arms when issuing invitations. Instead, women use their husband's crests or another device called a lozenge, which is a diamond-shaped symbol in which her family's coat of arms is combined with her husband's.

When used on a wedding invitation, the coat of arms is always blind-embossed at the top of the invitation. Blind-embossing requires an engraving die. If your family does not already have a die, you will need to allow extra time—sometimes up to 6 to 8 weeks—to have one made.

My father has a Ph.D. Does he use "Doctor" on my wedding invitations?

Ph.D. is an academic title that is used only in academic settings. The use of "Doctor" on wedding invitations is reserved for medical doctors and ministers with advanced degrees.

My father is a minister. How should my parents' names read?

The host line should read, "The Reverend and Mrs. Andrew Jay Forrester." A minister who holds a doctorate uses "The Reverend Doctor Andrew Jay Forrester." Neither "Reverend" nor "Doctor" should be abbreviated. If the host line becomes too long, it may be split to read "The Reverend Doctor / and Mrs. Andrew Jay Forrester."

My mother is a minister but my father is not. How do their names read?

Women traditionally use their social titles on social invitations so your parents' names should read, "Mr. and Mrs. Andrew Jay Forrester." If your mother chooses to use her theological title, the first line should read, "The Reverend Mary Chance Forrester." Your father's name would appear on the second line, which would read, "and Mr. Andrew Jay Forrester."

Both my parents are ministers. How should their names read?

Traditionally, your mother would use her social title on social invitations so that the host line would read "The Reverend and Mrs. Andrew Jay Forrester." However, if your mother chooses to use her theological title, the first line should read "The Reverend Mary Chance Forrester." Your father's name and title would appear on the second line preceded by "and."

My father is a judge. Does he use "The Honorable"?

"The Honorable" is always used when addressing a judge. However, when a judge issues an invitation, he does not use "The Honorable" since it would be presumptuous for him to bestow that title upon himself. He may use "Judge" as his title.

My mother is a judge but my father is not. How is that indicated?

If your mother chooses to use her professional title, her name would appear on the first line of the invitation preceded by "Judge." The second would read, "and Mr. Andrew Jay Forrester."

My fiancé and I are paying for the wedding. How is that indicated?

If you issue your wedding invitations yourselves, your guests will probably assume that you and your fiancé are paying for the wedding. You may also have your parents issue the invitations to the ceremony while you and your fiancé issue the invitations to the reception. The reception card would have your name and title on the first line and your fiancé's name and title on the second line. The rest of the reception card would read, "request the pleasure of your company / at the marriage reception / immediately following the ceremony" followed by the name of the facility at which the reception will be held.

My father dislikes his middle name. Is it proper to use his middle initial?

Formal wedding invitations require the use of full names, and never initials. If your father insists on not using his middle name, it's best to simply omit it entirely.

My father's middle name is just an initial. Is it proper to use his initial?

As long as the initial is truly his full middle name, it may be used.

My fiancé and I are older and have no need for any more gifts. How can we let our guests know that their gifts are not necessary?

While many couples do not feel that gifts are necessary, many guests do. Asking them to not give you gifts deprives them of an opportunity to share their love with you. (It may also seem presumptuous.) Besides, the types of gifts that are given to older couples are different from those given to young brides. You may find yourselves as pleased with your presents as your guests are with giving them.

We would like our guests to donate the money they would otherwise have spent on gifts to our favorite charity. How is that indicated?

Unfortunately, there is no tactful way of doing that. While enclosing a card reading, "In lieu of gifts we ask that you send a donation to the Special Olympics" may seem to you to be an innocent enough request it may be seen by others as presumptuous.

It is not considered polite to let your guests know that you expect anything from them—except the pleasure of their company.

Divorced Parents

Some of the most difficult situations in wording wedding invitations occur when the parents of the bride are divorced. There are simple and straightforward rules to handle these situations but sometimes emotions take control of circumstances and render these rules inadequate. You may find yourself unable to follow the prescribed rules of etiquette to a tee for fear of offending a family member or creating additional, unnecessary tensions. If you find yourself in this situation, you may choose to go a different route and find wording that is both appropriate and innocuous. Etiquette is intended as a guide to good taste and to facilitate good relationships and the comfort of everyone. Therefore, in such an instance it is entirely appropriate for you to stray from the accepted rules.

The proper way to word an invitation when the bride's parents are divorced is to list the names of the bride's parents at the top of the invitation. Her mother's name is on the first line and her father's name is on the line beneath it. The lines are not separated by "and."

My parents are divorced and my mother has not remarried. How should her name appear?

In instances where the bride's mother had taken her former husband's name during marriage and has not remarried, she uses either "Mrs." or "Ms." followed by her first name, maiden name, and married name. The old etiquette called for using just her maiden name and her last name, preceded by "Mrs." The change evolved over the years as it was increasingly felt that the old usage was too impersonal.

My mother has remarried. How should her name appear?

When the bride's mother is divorced from the bride's father and has remarried and taken a new name, she uses "Mrs." followed by her current husband's full name.

My parents are divorced and my father has remarried. Where does his wife's name appear?

Traditionally, you are "given away" by your parents. Therefore, it is generally only the names of your natural parents that properly appear on your wedding invitations. However, you may choose to set your own course for handling this matter by having your mother's name with a social title, either "Mrs." or "Ms.", appear on the first line. Your father and his new bride can be represented on the second line with "Mr. and Mrs." followed by your father's name. Your father's new wife's first name should not appear.

My mother was widowed when I was young and remarried. While I was never adopted by my stepfather, he did raise me. May I include his name on the invitation?

Yes. If a stepfather or stepmother essentially acted as a parent to you, it is appropriate for his or her name to appear on the invitations.

I'm afraid that if I don't include the name of my father's wife on my invitations, it might hurt her feelings.

Etiquette should never be adhered to at the cost of damaging a relationship. Its purpose is to build relationships, not to harm them. There are ways to handle any situation that will accommodate everybody involved.

Many brides choose to have their mother's name on the first line followed by a second line reading "Mr. and Mrs." followed by the father's name. Again, the word "and" is not used to join the two lines.

Both of my parents have remarried and I'm close to both stepparents. Can I include them on the invitation?

Again, it is your choice to follow or not follow the strict rules of etiquette. If you are more interested in including your extended family on your invitation than adhering to tradition, by all means do so.

This type of wording is often handled by listing the mother and her new husband's name on the first line and presented as "Mr. and Mrs." The father and his new wife's names appear on the second line as "Mr. and Mrs." The word "and" is typically not used to join the two lines but if relations between the couples are good and you feel it's appropriate, you may include it.

My parents are divorced and my father is paying for the wedding. How is that indicated?

Wedding invitations are worded the way they are to reflect the tradition of the bride's family graciously giving away the bride while inviting family and friends to join them for this happy occasion. As with the ceremony itself, the center of attention is the bride and groom. (That's why their names are spread out in the center of the invitation.) Therefore, there is no place to indicate who is paying the bills. To do so would be to draw attention away from the bride and groom.

If, after this explanation, you still feel a need to let people know that your father is picking up the tab, you may do so on the reception cards. The reception cards serve as invitations to the reception. By listing your father as host of the reception, you will be indicating to your guests that he is paying for it. This way, you have properly worded wedding invitations and reception cards that convey to your guests the fact that your father is funding the wedding.

Instead of reading, "Reception / immediately following the ceremony," your reception cards should read, "Mr. Andrew Jay Forrester / requests the pleasure of your company / at the marriage reception" followed by the date, time, and place.

My mother is divorced and has resumed using her maiden name. What title should she use?

Depending upon your and your mother's preference, her name may appear without a title or with "Ms." preceding it. When "Ms." is not used, all other titles should be omitted so that the invitation retains a uniform appearance.

Why isn't "and" used between the names of divorced parents?

By using "and" between the names of divorced parents, you create an additional line and a competing center of attention. The extra line draws your eye to both the top of the invitation and the center. It should be drawn directly to the center where the names of the bride and groom appear.

Separated Parents

When the bride's parents are legally separated, they may issue their daughter's wedding invitations together. Their names appear on separate lines with the name of the bride's mother on the first line and the bride's father's name on the second line. The word "and" is not used to join their names. Because they are separated but not divorced, the bride's mother's name should appear as it did when she was married. If she took her husband's name at marriage, it would appear as "Mrs." followed by her husband's name. If she is not comfortable with this, she may use her own full name preceded by "Mrs." or "Ms." Another option is to have her name appear without any title. This approach, however, requires the dropping of all other titles on the invitation in order to keep the rest of the invitation uniform.

Widowed Parents

When one of the bride's parents is deceased, her wedding invitations are issued by her surviving parent. Traditionally, his or her name appears alone on the host line. In most cases, stepparents' names are not used (see *below* for exceptions to this rule).

A widow retains the use of her husband's name. If she has not remarried, she continues to be known as "Mrs." Andrew Jay Forrester. If she has remarried, she uses "Mrs." followed by her present husband's name. In this case, since the bride's surname is different from her mother's surname, the bride's full name appears on the fourth line of the invitation. The bride's name is not preceded by "Miss."

Mrs. John Michael Davies

requests the honour of your presence

at the marriage of her daughter

Jennifer Marie Forrester

etc.

Including Stepparents on Invitations

An exception to the "no stepparents" rule occurs when the bride's mother or father remarried and the bride's stepparent helped raise the bride from a young age, and the bride feels especially close to her stepparent. In these situations, the name of the bride's stepparent may properly appear. When this is done, the third line of the invitation reads "at the marriage of her (his) daughter." This suggests to your guests that, in this case, your mother is your natural parent.

Mr. and Mrs. John Michael Davies

request the honour of your presence

at the marriage of her daughter

Jennifer Marie Forrester

etc.

When is it appropriate to use "senior"?

A man who is a "junior" usually stops using "junior" upon his father's death. If he is married, his widowed mother uses "senior" to distinguish herself from her daughter-in-law. "Senior" should be spelled out using a lowercase s. It may be abbreviated to "Sr." when used with an especially long name.

My mother is a widow who has not remarried. She prefers the use of her first name. Can her name read, "Mrs. Mary Chance Forrester"?

A widow who has not remarried should use her deceased husband's name, preceded by "Mrs." (A divorced woman uses "Mrs." followed by her first, maiden, and married names.) If your mother would rather use her first name, she can use "Ms." as a title or her name may appear without any title. The appearance of her name without titles makes the invitation slightly less formal and requires that all other titles be left off the invitation as well.

My father passed away last year and I would like to include his name on my wedding invitations. How is that done?

While wishing to include a deceased parent's name on a wedding invitation is a lovely sentiment, it is not proper to do so (except in Latin America). The essential purpose of a wedding invitation is to invite your guests to your wedding and to tell them where and when it is taking place. It lists the host or hosts of the event, what the event is (your wedding), and the date, time, and place. The only logical place to list your father's name is on the host line. This, however, would indicate he is one of the hosts of your wedding and would be inappropriate given he is deceased.

Your father's name is, of course, mentioned in your newspaper announcement and may also be mentioned in the wedding program and during a prayer said during the service. Your wedding is a joyous occasion. Reminding your guests of your father's death by adding "and the late Mr. Andrew Jay Forrester" introduces an element of sadness to an otherwise joyous occasion.

The Hispanic tradition, on the other hand, does include the name of a deceased parent. If the deceased parent is the bride's father, her mother's name appears alone on the first line and her father's name, followed by a small cross if Christian or a Star of David if Jewish, appears on line two. One note of caution: Your guests may not be familiar with this custom and may not understand the meaning of it. If you are planning to have a wedding program, this would be an ideal place to explain the symbols and their meaning.

Mrs. John Carlos Aponte

Mr. John Carlos Aponte †

request the honour of your presence

at the marriage of their daughter

etc.

Parents are in the Military

Invitations to weddings involving members of the United States armed services follow the same general guidelines used for civilian weddings. The format and the wording are the same. The only difference is in the use of titles. While civilians use social titles such as "Mr.," "Mrs.," and the professional title of "Doctor" for medical doctors, military personnel use their military titles, which many times include their rank and branch of service. Military titles should not be abbreviated. (See page 77 for examples.)

Second Marriages

According to many studies, about half of all Americans will divorce and remarry. Subsequently, a growing number of wedding invitations issued today involve a bride or groom marrying for a second time. When either the bride or both the bride and the groom are marrying for the second time, the wedding invitations are issued by the bride and groom themselves. A bride who is being married for the first time to a groom who is marrying for the second time, typically, has her invitations issued by her parents. In other words, it is the bride's status that determines the wording of the invitation. The groom's previous marital status does not affect the invitations.

Traditionally, a divorced bride marrying for the second time used her first name, maiden name, and married name preceded by "Mrs." on her wedding invitations. Through the years, this has changed as the great majority of brides have felt that the inclusion of "Mrs." on their wedding invitations was unnecessary and inappropriate. Today, it is entirely appropriate not to use "Mrs." and almost every bride chooses to omit it.

Whenever the bride's title is omitted, the groom's title is also omitted. This keeps the wording of the invitations consistent.

If the bride resumed use of her maiden name after her divorce, no social title should be used.

Widows marrying again properly use "Mrs." followed by their deceased husband's name. A young widow, however, may have her parents issue her invitations, even if they issued the invitations to her first wedding. A young widow uses her first, maiden, and married names. No title is used.

The most formal wording for a second marriage omits the host line. A less formal, but still correct wording places the bride's and groom's names at the top of the invitation.

My parents sent traditional invitations for my first wedding. Is it proper for me to send traditional invitations for my second wedding?

Wedding invitations set the tone for the wedding, regardless of whether it is a first, second, or third wedding. If your wedding is going to be a traditional one, you should send traditional invitations.

If the tone is less formal, choose a format and style that reflects that. The most important thing is that the invitation captures the spirit of the event you are planning and the joy of the union.

DIVORCED BRIDE:

The honour of your presence

is requested at the marriage of

Jennifer Forrester Neal

to Nicholas Jude Strickland

etc.

OR:

Jennifer Marie Forrester

and

Nicholas Jude Strickland

request the honour of your presence

at their marriage

etc.

WIDOWED BRIDE:

The honour of your presence

is requested at the marriage of

Mrs. James Richard Celestino

to

Mr. Nicholas Jude Strickland

etc.

Some etiquette books claim that it is not proper to have invitations to a second wedding engraved. Is this true?

The quality inherent to engraving exists whether you are marrying for the first or second time. There is no reason why the invitations to your second wedding cannot be engraved. If you appreciate the quality of engraving, then by all means have them engraved.

I am marrying for the third time. How should my name read?

Your first name, maiden name, and your second husband's last name are used. You can use "Mrs." as your social title or omit a title entirely. Your first husband's name should be omitted entirely.

I am divorced and getting remarried. May I use "Ms." instead of "Mrs."?

"Ms." serves the same function for women that "Mr." does for men. It may be used with either the last name alone or with the full name. Like "Mr.", "Ms." does not denote marital status and may be properly used by both single and married women.

I am a doctor. Is it proper for me to use my title?

If you are a medical doctor, you may use your title on your wedding invitations. Your title precedes your name and no advanced degrees appear after it. "Doctor" should be spelled out, not abbreviated. Ph.D.s do not properly use their academic title.

My first wedding was an elopement. This time around I am going to have a traditional wedding hosted by my parents. How should my invitations read?

Your wedding invitations read as if this were your first wedding, except for your name. Instead of just your given names, your first, maiden, and married names are used.

My first marriage was annulled. How should my wedding invitations read?

An annulment makes a marriage null and void. Therefore, you are entitled to use your maiden name. On invitations issued by your parents, your full maiden name is used, not just your given names. Your maiden name, preceded by "Miss," is used on invitations issued by you and your fiancé. Titles may also be left off invitations that you and your fiancé issue.

We are both marrying for the second time and have no need for any more gifts. How can we let our guests know that their gifts are not necessary?

While many couples do not feel that gifts are necessary, many guests do. Asking them to not give you gifts deprives them of an opportunity to share their love with you. (It may also seem presumptuous.) Besides, the types of gifts that are given to older couples are different from those given to young brides and grooms. You may find yourselves as pleased with your presents as your guests are with giving them.

We would like our guests to donate the money they would otherwise have spent on gifts to our favorite charity. How is that indicated?

Unfortunately, there is no tactful way of doing that. While enclosing a card reading, "In lieu of gifts we ask that you send a donation to the Special Olympics" may seem to you to be an innocent enough request, it may be seen by others as presumptuous.

It is considered impolite to let your guests know that you expect anything from them—except the pleasure of their company.

Invitations Issued by the Couple

Although it is considered most proper for the parents of the bride to issue their daughter's wedding invitations, there may be times when the couple chooses to issue the invitations themselves. This most commonly occurs when the bride's parents are deceased, when the couple is older, the ceremony is a same-sex union, or when one of the couple is marrying for the second time.

There are two proper formats for self-invitations. The more formal of the two contains no host line. The less formal format lists both the bride and groom as hosts.

The honour of your presence

is requested at the marriage of

Miss Jennifer Marie Forrester

to

Mr. Nicholas Jude Strickland

etc.

OR:

Miss Jennifer Marie Forrester

and

Mr. Nicholas Jude Strickland

request the honour of your presence

etc.

Although my fiancé and I are not medical doctors now, we will be before our wedding. Is it proper for us to use "doctor" on our invitations?

Since you will be medical doctors on the day you are married, it is proper for you to use your new title.

My fiancé and I are paying for our wedding. How is that indicated?

If your parents are alive, your wedding invitation is most properly issued in their name regardless of who is paying. Some family circumstances, however, will necessitate an exception to that rule. If your parents' names

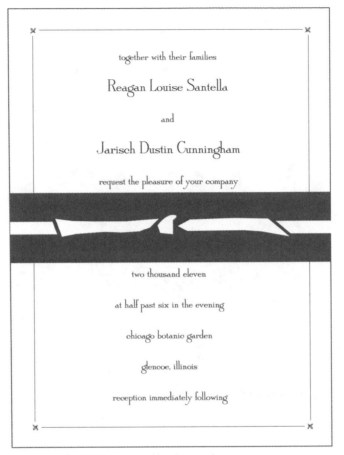

together with their families

Reagan Louise Santella

and

Jarisch Dustin Cunningham

request the pleasure of your company

two thousand eleven

at half past six in the evening

chicago botanic garden

glencoe, illinois

reception immediately following

▲ Sample of an invitation issued by the couple

are not mentioned, most people will assume that the two of you are paying for your wedding.

Invitations Issued by the Groom's Parents

On rare occasions, perhaps when the bride's parents are deceased or when they live in a foreign country, the groom's parents may issue the wedding invitations. The format is a little different from the standard format. The parents' relationship to the groom is mentioned on the fifth line of the invitation instead of on the third line. This way, the invitations can still be read as the bride being married to the groom. Both the bride and the groom use their full names, preceded by their titles.

Mr. and Mrs. John Peter Strickland

request the honour of your presence

at the marriage of

Miss Jennifer Marie Forrester

to their son

Mr. Nicholas Jude Strickland

etc.

Invitations Issued by Other Relatives

Any member of the bride's family may host her wedding and issue the invitations when the bride's parents are deceased. The bride's relationship to her relatives issuing the invitation is designated on the third line of the invitation where the word "daughter" normally appears. The bride's full name minus her title appears on the following line.

Mr. and Mrs. David Allen Forrester

request the honour of your presence

at the marriage of their granddaughter

Jennifer Marie Forrester

etc.

Invitations Issued by Friends of the Bride

Friends of the bride may issue wedding invitations when the bride's parents are deceased and she has no close relatives. When friends issue the invitations, no relationship is shown on the third line and the bride's full name, preceded by "Miss," appears on the following line.

Mr. and Mrs. Charles Douglas Goldman

request the honour of your presence

at the marriage of

Miss Jennifer Marie Forrester

etc.

Request Lines

The request line invites your guests to your ceremony. The wording varies according to where the event is being held. The correct wording for a wedding held in a church, temple, synagogue, or any house of worship is, "request the honour of your presence." The word "honour" is used to show deference to God whenever a wedding is held in a house of worship. For weddings held in any location other than a house of worship, "request the pleasure of your company" is used.

Which is more formal: "request the honour of your presence" or "request the pleasure of your company"?
Both phrases are equal in their formality. They are just used under different circumstances.

What is the correct spelling of "honor"?
Both "honour" and "honor" are correct. It is a matter of personal preference, although the vast majority of brides prefer the English spelling, "honour."

UPDATED: *Commitment Ceremonies*

Same-sex ceremonies are not held to the same etiquette standards as traditional male-female weddings, thus offering the couple considerable flexibility in the wording of their invitation. The event is often referred to as a commitment ceremony, a union ceremony, a marriage ceremony, a wedding ceremony, and often as simply a celebration. The best course of action is to choose the phrase that best represents how you view the event.

My wedding is being held at home and is a religious ceremony. May I use "request the honour of your presence"?

The use of "request the honour of your presence" is reserved for weddings held on sanctified ground, so it is not properly used for a wedding held at home.

Bride's Name

The bride's given names are used on invitations issued by her parents. Neither her social title nor her last name is used since it is assumed that she has never married and has the same last name as her parents. If her last name is different from her parents' last name, she includes her last name on her invitations.

I am a medical doctor. May I use "doctor"?

If you are a medical doctor, your title may appear on your wedding invitations. Your title precedes your name and no advanced degrees appear after it. "Doctor" should be spelled out, not abbreviated. Ph.D.s do not properly use their academic title.

I am in the military. May I use my rank?

Yes, military titles should be included on your invitation. Titles should never be abbreviated. Your branch of service should be listed on the line below your name.

IF THE BRIDE-TO-BE IS IN THE SERVICE:

Lieutenant Colonel and Mrs. William Matthew Hoag

request the honour of your presence

at the marriage of their daughter

Captain Marissa Lynne Hoag

United States Air Force

to

Mr. Derek Hunter Healy

etc.

I am an attorney. May I use "esquire"?

While some lawyers have adopted "esquire" as a title to designate their status as attorneys, "esquire" is not recognized as a proper title for social invitations in the United States. In England, the title means "gentleman" and is used to honor a man when addressing him and therefore would not be an appropriate reference for a woman under any circumstance.

I was adopted. Is that mentioned on my wedding invitations?

No. The parents who raised you issue your invitations and your adoption is not mentioned.

Why are the names of the bride and groom larger than the rest of the copy?

Actually, all the proper names (the bride, groom, bride's parents, and the church) on a wedding invitation are highlighted since these are the most important lines. The names of the bride and groom stand out even more because of the very short line ("to" or "and") that separates them.

Joining Word

The joining word is the word that joins the names of the couple. The preposition "to" is used on invitations to the wedding ceremony as the bride is traditionally married to the groom. The conjunction "and" is used on invitations to the reception since the reception is given in honor of the couple. "And" is also used on Jewish wedding invitations, for Nuptial Masses, and on invitations issued by the couple.

Groom's Name

Traditionally, the groom always uses his full name, preceded by his title. If, however, the parents' names are not preceded by titles, the couple may choose to drop it from the groom's name for the sake of consistency.

There are no abbreviations, except for "Mr." All other titles, such as "Doctor" and "The Reverend" should be written out, although "Doctor" may be abbreviated when used with a long name. If "Doctor" is used more than once on an invitation, its use should be consistent. If it is necessary to abbreviate it with one of the names, it should be abbreviated with all names.

Initials are never properly used on formal wedding invitations. Men who dislike their middle names and use their middle initial instead should be discouraged from doing so. If your fiancé declines to use his middle name, it is better to omit his middle name entirely than to use just his initial.

Can "junior" be abbreviated or must it be spelled out?

Properly, "junior" is written out. Abbreviating "junior" to "Jr." is less formal but still acceptable. When written out, a lowercase j is used. When abbreviated, the J is capitalized. The abbreviation is commonly used when the groom has an exceptionally long name. A comma always precedes "junior," whether written out or abbreviated.

My fiancé is a "junior." His father, however, has passed away. Does my fiancé continue to use "junior"?

Since your fiancé and his father shared the same last name, your fiancé used "junior" to distinguish himself from his father. Now that his father has passed away, he no longer needs to use "junior" and may drop it from his name. Of course, if either your fiancé or his father was a well-known public or private figure, your fiancé would continue to use "junior" to avoid any confusion.

When are "II" and "III" properly used?

Although it may seem as though "junior" and the "II" can be used interchangeably, they are actually different designations. "Junior" is used by a man whose father has the same name that he has, whereas the "II" is used by a man who has the same name as the older relative (usually a grandfather) other than the father.

The "III" is used by the namesake of a man using "junior" or "II." When used on an invitation, a comma usually precedes the "II" or "III." Some men prefer to omit the comma. Either way is correct.

My fiancé is a doctor. Does his title appear on our invitations?

Medical doctors properly use their professional titles on wedding invitations, whereas Ph.D.s do not. The word "Doctor" should be spelled out unless your fiancé's name is exceptionally long.

Medical degrees, such as M.D. or D.D.S. are never mentioned. They are professional designations and therefore do not belong on a social invitation. Their use should be reserved for business cards and professional letterheads.

My fiancé is in the military. How should his rank appear on our invitations?

Your fiancé's title should appear before his name. Military titles should never be abbreviated. Your fiancé's branch of service should appear on the line below his name.

My fiancé is a lawyer. May he use "esquire"?

While some lawyers have adopted "esquire" as a title to designate their status as attorneys, "esquire" is not recognized as a proper title for social invitations in the United States. In England, the title means "gentleman" and is used to honor a man when addressing him. For a man to bestow that designation upon himself is considered presumptuous and in poor taste.

My fiancé is known by his nickname. Since none of our friends know his real name, would it be appropriate to put his nickname in parentheses?

Nicknames are never properly used on traditional wedding invitations. The names on your fiancé's birth certificate should be used.

IF THE GROOM-TO-BE IS IN THE SERVICE:

Mr. and Mrs. Frederick Michael Barber

request the honour of your presence

at the marriage of their daughter

Catherine Louise

to

John Patrick Wyman

Lieutenant, United States Army

etc.

Date Line

The day of the week and the date are written out in full. Abbreviations are not used. For some styles of invitations, the use of numerals rather than spelled-out numbers is more appropriate. The day of the week is first, followed by the date of the month and the month itself. The day of the week may be preceded by "on." The use of "on," however, is unnecessary and may make the line too long.

You may include the time of day, as in, "Saturday evening." That is not usually necessary, however, as most people are able to determine whether your invitation is for the morning or evening without specifically being told. For example, an invitation reading, "at six o'clock" is obviously meant for six o'clock in the evening. If that invitation were meant for six o'clock in the morning, it would then be necessary to include "Saturday morning" since that would be unusual.

Invitations for weddings held at eight, nine, or ten o'clock should designate morning or evening since weddings are held at those times during both mornings and evenings. Many Roman Catholic weddings, for example, are held at those times in the mornings since most Nuptial Masses are held before noon, while some Jewish weddings are held at those times on Saturday evenings so the guests and participants can wait until after sundown to travel on the Sabbath.

The time of day can be noted on the time line instead.

Year Line

Since wedding invitations are sent four to six weeks before the wedding, it is not necessary to include the year. Your guests will assume that the invitation is for the next August twenty-third and not for some other August twenty-third in the distant future.

Although it is not necessary to include the year, it is not improper to do so. Your invitations will, undoubtedly, be saved by family and friends as a remembrance and may even be passed down to your children, grandchildren, and great-grandchildren. Including the year on your invitation will help your descendants remember your wedding day.

There are a couple of cautions, though, about including the year. First, many lettering styles, especially some of the script lettering styles, look better with fewer lines of copy. Additional lines might make your invitation look too cluttered.

Second, the year line is a long, heavy line that follows two other heavy lines (the groom's name and the date). This creates a lot of weight in that part of the invitation, which can draw your eye there instead of to the names of the bride and groom, where it should be drawn.

Wedding announcements, on the other hand, are sent after the wedding has taken place. Therefore, it is necessary to include the year or it could be assumed that your wedding took place on any August twenty-third in the past.

Should the T in "two thousand" be upper– or lowercase?

Although both ways are proper and many older invitations use all lowercase letters on the year line, almost all invitations nowadays capitalize the first letter. This usage is so common that not to do it might make it look as though your stationer forgot to capitalize the first letter. Furthermore, your invitations will look more polished if the first letter of the year is capitalized.

Time Line

An old superstition claims that being married on the half hour brings good fortune since the minute hand is ascending toward heaven, while being married on the hour leads to a bad marriage since, as with the minute hand, it is all downhill from there. Perhaps it is best to be married at noon when both hands are in the praying position.

No matter what the specific hour, the time of the wedding is presented on one line and all letters are lowercase. If your wedding is being held at six o'clock, the time line simply reads, "at six o'clock." The time line for weddings held at six-thirty reads, "at half after six o'clock."

The time line can be used to designate the time of day by using either "in the morning, "in the afternoon," or "in the evening." For most times it is not usually necessary, since a wedding held at six o'clock is obviously being held in the evening. Weddings held at eight, nine, or ten o'clock are another matter, since they could be held in the morning or the evening. In those cases, a designation denoting the time of day is helpful. In any event, you may include the time of day, as was done in the past, if you find it aesthetically pleasing.

My wedding is being held at noon. Should my invitations read "at twelve o'clock noon"?

Your invitations should simply read, "at twelve o'clock." Unless otherwise noted, "twelve o'clock" means "noon."

If you feel strongly about indicating the time of day, you may use, "at twelve o'clock in the afternoon."

I am being married at 6:45. How should this be read?

The correct wording for 6:45 is "at three quarters after six o'clock." Although correct, the wording may appear awkward to many people, so it might be a good idea to change the time of your wedding to six-thirty or seven o'clock.

Location

Wedding ceremonies are held at a variety of locations including churches, temples, synagogues, clubs, and even at home. The location line tells your guests the name of the location at which your wedding is being held. The full name of the facility is always given, so the location line for the wedding held at a church, for example, uses the full corporate name of the church.

There should be no abbreviations. "Saint" is always spelled out. Likewise, a church commonly referred to as "Saint Matthew's Church" might actually be "Church of Saint Matthew" or "Saint Matthew's Roman Catholic Church." You should check with a clergyman or the church secretary to ascertain the correct name of the church.

My parents are hosting my wedding at home. How is that indicated?

While most wedding ceremonies are held in churches, hotels, and country clubs, many are held at home. The ceremony can be a religious one or a civil one. (Some religions, however, require that their wedding ceremonies be held in their place of worship.) The location given is simply your parents' address. Since your wedding is taking place outside a house of worship, "request the pleasure of your company" is used.

We are having a garden wedding at my parents' home. Should our invitations indicate that it will be a garden wedding?

It is always helpful to mention that the wedding will be a garden wedding to ensure that your guests wear appropriate footwear. A line reading, "in the garden" appears above your parents' address.

Our wedding is being held at a friend's house. How does the location line read?

Your friend's name and address are shown at the end of the invitation.

Our wedding is being held in a small chapel at the Church of Christ. Is that noted on the invitations?

The name of the chapel may be given on the line directly above the name of the church. Your wording should begin with the specifics of the location (i.e. chapel or room) and move to the more general (i.e. church or hall) from there.

Street Address

The accepted rule on the use of the street address is that its inclusion is optional unless there is more than one facility with that name in that town, in which case it is mandatory. The street address is also used when the facility is not well known or when there are a number of out-of-town guests. Since giving the street address is an additional courtesy to your guests, it is almost always proper. The only time its use is not proper is when direction and map cards are used. Then the street address is redundant. Including the street address, however, adds an extra line to the invitation. Most invitations, especially those engraved in script lettering styles, look better with fewer lines of copy, so before you decide to include the address consider the aesthetics.

City and State

The last line in the main body of the invitation shows the names of the city and state in which your wedding is being held. Both city and state are included, and are separated by a comma.

Two exceptions to this rule are New York City and Washington, D.C. For weddings held in New York, "New York City" or just "New York" are used since "New York, New York" seems redundant. The city and state line for weddings held in Washington, D.C., can read "City of Washington" or "Washington, District of Columbia."

Wedding and Reception Held at the Same Place

When a wedding ceremony and reception are held in the same location, a line reading either "and afterwards at the reception" or "and afterward at the reception" is included on the invitations. This line appears at the end of the body of the invitation, beneath the city and state.

ROOTED IN TRADITION: *Rain Cards*

One of the risks involved in having an outdoor wedding is that you are at the mercy of the elements. You may enclose a small "rain card" with your invitations that reads, "In case of inclement weather / the wedding will be held at / Sleepy Hollow Country Club / Scarborough." Of course, all of your guests will have different definitions of inclement weather. A cloudy wedding day may produce a very large number of phone calls. If you are planning an outdoor wedding, a tent would be a much wiser investment than a bad-weather enclosed card.

Mr. and Mrs. Andrew Jay Forrester

request the pleasure of your company

at the marriage of their daughter

Jennifer Marie

to

Nicholas Jude Strickland

Saturday, the twenty-third of August

at six o'clock

at the residence of

Mr. and Mrs. Michael Anthony LaPointe

217 Old Orchard Road

Bedford, New York

and afterwards at the reception

My wedding and reception are being held at the same place. I do not want to send reply cards but I do not like the way corner lines look on wedding invitations. How should my reception cards read?

Although reception cards are not necessary in your situation, they may be used to convey your reply information. The reception cards read as they would if your reception were being held elsewhere. The name of the facility and its address, however, may be omitted since they are already given on the invitations.

RELIGIOUS AND CULTURAL CONSIDERATIONS

Roman Catholic Weddings

The Roman Catholic Church requires the posting of banns, the public announcement of a couple's intentions to marry. The banns must be announced from the pulpit or in the church bulletin three times before the wedding. The traditional posting of the banns was the forerunner of wedding announcements in the newspaper.

Catholics can be married in a simple wedding service or in a Nuptial Mass. A Nuptial Mass is a wedding ceremony performed as part of the Catholic Mass (or service). When the wedding ceremony will be a Nuptial Mass, the invitations should mention that a Nuptial Mass will be performed. Nuptial Masses are about an hour long. Placing the phrase "Nuptial Mass" on the wedding invitations alerts guests to the fact that the wedding will take a little longer than what they might be accustomed to.

Mr. and Mrs. Andrew Jay Forrester

request the honour of your presence

at the Nuptial Mass uniting their daughter

Jennifer Marie

and

Mr. Nicholas Jude Strickland

Saturday, the twenty-third of August

at nine o'clock in the morning

Saint Matthew's Roman Catholic Church

Scarborough, New York

Nuptial Masses were once performed only at or before noon but are now performed in the afternoon as well. Unless special permission is granted by the bishop, Nuptial Masses may not be performed during Lent or Advent.

As suggested by the invitations, the bride and groom are joined together in holy matrimony. Therefore, "and" is used instead of "to."

Jewish Weddings

According to Jewish tradition, marriages are made in heaven. Men and women are brought together to marry one another by God Himself. Women are not married "to" men. Rather, men and women are joined together in marriage. Because of this tradition, the joining word on Jewish wedding invitations reads "and" instead of "to."

Jewish custom also celebrates the joining of the two families, so the names of the groom's parents always appear on the invitations. Their names most properly appear beneath the groom's name and a line reading "son of Mr. and Mrs. Solomon Lang" or on two lines that read, "son of / Mr. and Mrs. Solomon Lang." Their names may also appear at the top of the invitations beneath the names of the bride's parents. This is done occasionally by parents of the bride who feel that they honor the groom's parents more by placing their names at the top of the invitation. When this is done, the request line reads, "at the marriage of." The bride, in this case, uses her full name but no title. The groom's title is omitted as well to maintain uniformity.

Hebrew lettering is often used on Jewish wedding invitations. It may take the form of a quotation from the wedding blessing, blind-embossed across the top of the invitation, or the entire invitation text may be reproduced in Hebrew on a part of the invitation. When the invitation appears in both English and Hebrew, the Hebrew version appears on the left-inside page while the English version appears on the right-inside page.

UPDATED: *Wedding Programs*

Programs are particularly helpful for guests at interfaith marriages or any time the guest list includes a number of people who may not be familiar with the rituals and traditions of a Jewish ceremony.

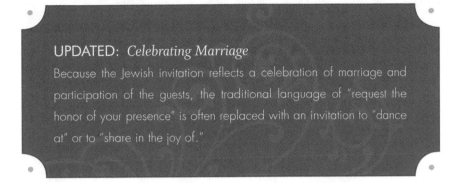

UPDATED: *Celebrating Marriage*

Because the Jewish invitation reflects a celebration of marriage and participation of the guests, the traditional language of "request the honor of your presence" is often replaced with an invitation to "dance at" or to "share in the joy of."

For reform couples, in lieu of full Hebrew text, many invitations will simply have their names written in Hebrew, next to the English version, or the date of the wedding in Hebrew.

Mr. and Mrs. David Green

request the honour of your presence

at the marriage of their daughter

Deborah

to

Mr. Steven Lang

son of

Mr. and Mrs. Solomon Lang

Sunday, the twenty-fourth of August

at six o'clock

Temple Beth-el

Scarsdale, New York

We're having an Orthodox service with a Hakhnassat Kallah (Bride's reception), a Chatan's Tish (Groom's reception), and a bedeken immediately prior to the service. What is the appropriate way to inform our guests of the start time for these pre-ceremonial events?

Because these events are being held at the same location as the wedding, you may mention these events directly on the invitation. Alternatively, an insert similar to a reception card may also be used to inform and invite your guests.

Is it proper to use "at the marriage of their children"?

While it is equally correct to use "at the marriage of their children" and "at the marriage of," many people feel that if a couple is old enough to get married, they are no longer children.

Mr. and Mrs. David Green

Mr. and Mrs. Solomon Lang

request the honour of your presence

at the marriage of

Deborah Ruth Green

and

Steven Matthew Lang

etc.

Mormon Weddings

Members of the Church of Jesus Christ of Latter-day Saints are married or "sealed" for "time and eternity" in temples open only to practicing Latter-day Saints. Weddings are generally small and intimate, attended by family and very close friends. The reception afterwards is a much larger affair to which all friends and all members of the bride's and groom's extended families are invited. Since more guests are invited to the reception than to the ceremony, the invitations are for the reception. Ceremony cards enclosed with the reception invitations are sent to those guests who are also invited to the temple ceremony.

Mr. and Mrs. Andrew Jay Forrester

request the pleasure of your company

at the marriage reception of their daughter

Jennifer Marie

and

Mr. Nicholas Jude Strickland

son of

Mr. and Mrs. John Peter Strickland

following their marriage

in the Salt Lake L.D.S. Temple

Saturday, the twenty-third of August

from seven until nine o'clock

La Caille at Quail Run

Salt Lake City, Utah

Invitations to Latter-day Saint wedding receptions differ from standard reception invitations in that they mention that the wedding ceremony was performed in the Latter-day Saint temple. Because Latter-day Saints place great emphasis on the importance of families, the groom's parents are honored by having their names mentioned on wedding invitations. Their names appear beneath the groom's name, preceded by "son of" on a separate line. Guests drop in and out of Latter-day Saint receptions. They arrive to congratulate the newlyweds and stay for a while to talk to friends and to renew acquaintances. Then they leave and go on their way. Consequently, the time line on the invitations mentions the time period during which the reception will be held.

Ceremony cards draw a distinction between weddings held in a Mormon temple and weddings held elsewhere. When weddings are held in a temple, it is so noted on the ceremony card.

Is it proper for us to send a photograph of ourselves with our wedding invitations?
It is very common in the Latter-day Saints community to include photographs with, or even feature them on, the invitations. While old rules of etiquette would deem photos superfluous, it is certainly considered acceptable and, in some circles, expected, to include them.

Hispanic Weddings

Traditional invitations to Hispanic weddings are issued by both sets of parents. The names of the bride's parents are always listed first.

Hispanic invitations can be done in a number of different formats. They may be produced on one page, in English or Spanish, with the names of the bride's parents listed separately on the first two lines, "and" on the third line, and the names of the groom's parents listed on the following two lines.

They may also be produced in both languages on the two inside pages of the invitations. The left inside page may appear in Spanish while the right inside page appears in English. When this format is used, the parents' names appear as described above.

Another frequently used format for Hispanic wedding invitations is an invitation where text appears on the two inside pages. The right inside page is an invitation from the groom's parents and the left-inside page is an invitation from the bride's parents. Common copy, such as date, time, and place, may be combined in the center of the invitation.

Customs may vary from one Latin American country to another. If you have any questions concerning the etiquette practiced in a particular country, it is best to call the protocol officer in their consulate for answers.

José Hernandez Caratini

Carmen Maria de Hernandez

y

Juan Martinez Garza

Consuela Elena de Martinez

tienen el honor de invitarle

al matrimonio de sus hijos

Linda

y

Roberto

el sabado diez de Julio

de mil novecientos noventa y siete

a las dos de la tarde

Santa Iglesia Catedral

San Juan de Puerto Rico

José Hernandez Caratini	*Juan Martinez Garza*
Carmen Maria de Hernandez	*Consuela Elena de Martinez*
request the honour of your presence	*request the honour of your presence*
at the marriage of their daughter	*at the marriage of*
Linda	*Linda Hernandez*
to	*to their son*
Roberto Martinez	*Roberto*

Saturday, the tenth of July
Two thousand ten
at two o'clock
Santa Iglesia Cathedral
San Juan, Puerto Rico

Indian Weddings

While Indian weddings may be conducted in the tradition of Hindu, Bengali, Kashmiri, Maharashtrian, Muslim, Punjabi, Gujarati, Arya Samaj, Telugu, Temil, or a combination of faiths, one consistent element is the rich and luxurious nature of the invitation.

A vibrant colored stock, very often a rich red or saffron, with an ornate border or motif reflecting the couple's Indian roots is traditional. It is not uncommon for Indian wedding invitations to be produced in a scroll format or even embellished with jewels. Invitations to any related dance parties or celebrations sometimes share elements of the wedding invitation but it is not necessary. Wording of the invitation varies depending upon the type of service being held. Couples should consult with their designated officiant for the specific language to be used on the invitation.

ROOTED IN TRADITION: *Issuance*

In traditional Indian culture, the invitation is issued by the elder in the family on the groom's father's side. That is, if the groom's grandfather on the father's side is alive, it goes out in his name. If he is deceased, then the grandmother is the issuer. If she is also deceased, it goes out in the groom's father's name. If he, too, is also deceased, it is issued in the name of the groom's mother.

Interfaith Marriages

Because interfaith marriages involve the blending of two sets of traditions and customs, there are no hard and fast rules for invitations. The most important thing is that the couple finds a way to reflect the nature of their union and service, while being respectful of each other's faiths.

Very often couples will use elements of the traditional wording and style of each faith on their invitation, thereby setting the tone and spirit of the union for their guests.

Bilingual Marriages

Bilingual invitations can be handled in any number of ways. Very often the invitation will appear in two columns, with the left column appearing in English and the right column in the second language appropriate for the family or guests of the bride and groom.

If space does not allow for a two-column format, a folded invitation can also be created with separate wording in the two native languages, facing one another.

Alternatively, a separate insert can be created in the second language and included with the reception card and other invitation elements.

MILITARY WEDDINGS

Invitations to weddings involving members of the United States armed services follow the same general guidelines used for civilian weddings. The format and the wording are the same. The only difference is in the use of titles. While civilians use social titles such as "Mr.," "Mrs.," and "Doctor," military personnel use their military titles, which many times include their rank and branch of service. Military titles should not be abbreviated.

Officers in the army, air force, and marines with a rank of captain or higher use their military titles before their names. Navy and coast guard officers with a rank of commander or higher also use their military titles before their names. When officers' names are used by themselves, the name of the branch of service in which they serve is mentioned on the line beneath their names. When their names are used with their spouse's name, the branch of service is not mentioned.

Junior officers do not use titles (neither military nor civilian) before their names. Their titles appear on a second line before the name of their branch of service. First lieutenants and Second lieutenants in the army both use "Lieutenant." In the air force and marines, however, "First" and "Second" are used.

All members of the military use only their branch of service on a second line. Their ranks are not used.

High-ranking officers who retire generally continue to use their titles. Their retired status is noted after their service designation. When the service designation is not used, as on invitations issued by a retired colonel and his wife, the officer's retired status is not mentioned.

ANNIVERSARIES, REAFFIRMATIONS, AND COMMITMENT CEREMONIES

Wedding Anniversaries

While wedding anniversaries are observed every year, major celebrations are usually reserved for the twenty-fifth, fortieth, and fiftieth anniversaries. While some traditional color guidelines may be followed in choosing an invitation—silver for a twenty-fifth anniversary, gold for a fiftieth—there are no hard and fast rules for choosing paper stock or ink. Invitation styles vary dramatically depending on the individuals being celebrated and the nature of the event. An invitation that best captures the spirit of the couple or the theme of the event makes for the best choice.

Military Titles on Invitations

	BRIDE'S NAME	GROOM'S NAME
OFFICER	Commander Jennifer Marie Forrester United States Army	Major Nicholas Jude Strickland United States Marine Corps
JUNIOR OFFICER	Jennifer Marie Forrester Ensign, United States Navy	Nicholas Jude Strickland First Lieutenant, United States Marine Corps
NONCOMMISSIONED OFFICER OR ENLISTED PERSON	Jennifer Marie Forrester United States Navy	Nicholas Jude Strickland United States Marine Corps

	BRIDE'S PARENTS (MARRIED)	BRIDE'S PARENTS (DIVORCED)
FATHER IS AN OFFICER	Colonel and Mrs. Andrew Jay Forrester	Mrs. Mary Chance Forrester Colonel Andrew Jay Forrester United States Army
FATHER IS A JUNIOR OFFICER	Lieutenant and Mrs. Andrew Jay Forrester	Mrs. Mary Chance Forrester Andrew Jay Forrester Lieutenant, United States Army
FATHER IS A NONCOMMISSIONED OFFICER OR ENLISTED MAN	Mr. and Mrs. Andrew Jay Forrester	Mrs. Mary Chance Forrester Andrew Jay Forrester United States Army
FATHER IS A RETIRED OFFICER	Colonel and Mrs. Andrew Jay Forrester	Mrs. Mary Chance Forrester Colonel Andrew Jay Forrester United States Army, Retired
MOTHER IS AN OFFICER	Mr. and Mrs. Andrew Jay Forrester or Captain Mary Chance Forrester United States Army and Mr. Andrew Jay Forrester	Captain Mary Chance Forrester United States Army Mr. Andrew Jay Forrester
BOTH PARENTS ARE OFFICERS	Colonel and Mrs. Andrew Jay Forrester or Captain Mary Chance Forrester/ United States Army/ and Colonel Andrew Jay Forrester/ United States Army	
PARENTS HOLD SAME RANK	Colonel and Mrs. Andrew Jay Forrester or The Colonels Forrester or Captain Mary Chance Forrester/ United States Army/ and Colonel Andrew Jay Forrester/ United States Army	

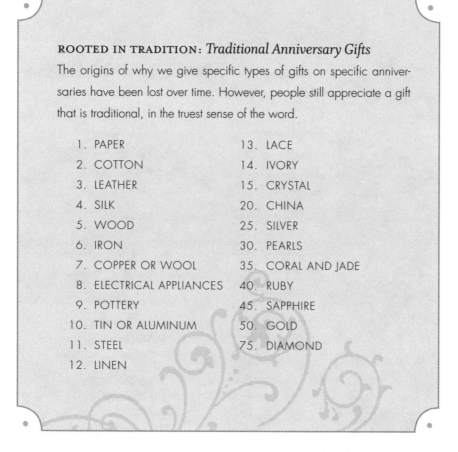

ROOTED IN TRADITION: *Traditional Anniversary Gifts*

The origins of why we give specific types of gifts on specific anniversaries have been lost over time. However, people still appreciate a gift that is traditional, in the truest sense of the word.

1. PAPER	13. LACE
2. COTTON	14. IVORY
3. LEATHER	15. CRYSTAL
4. SILK	20. CHINA
5. WOOD	25. SILVER
6. IRON	30. PEARLS
7. COPPER OR WOOL	35. CORAL AND JADE
8. ELECTRICAL APPLIANCES	40. RUBY
9. POTTERY	45. SAPPHIRE
10. TIN OR ALUMINUM	50. GOLD
11. STEEL	75. DIAMOND
12. LINEN	

Invitations to wedding anniversaries are usually extended by the couple's children and their spouses, but often friends, grandchildren, and even the couple themselves, may issue them as well. The years of the marriage are typically shown at the top of the invitation. Depending upon the format of the invitation, reply information may be included on the invitation or on a separate reply card.

1961 - 2011

Mr. and Mrs. Nicholas Jude Strickland, junior

Mr. and Mrs. Robert Stuart Strickland

Mr. and Mrs. John Kevin Murphey

request the pleasure of your company

at a dinner to celebrate

the Fiftieth Wedding Anniversary of

Mr. and Mrs. Nicholas Jude Strickland

Saturday, the second of April

at seven o'clock

Sleepy Hollow Country Club

Scarborough, New York

▲ Sample of an invitation to a wedding anniversary

Reaffirmation of Wedding Vows

A number of couples choose to celebrate their anniversaries by having a ceremony to renew their wedding vows. Other couples, married in a civil ceremony for one reason or another, choose to reaffirm their vows under religious auspices. As with any other invitation, invitations to reaffirmation ceremonies should reflect the level of formality of the occasion.

Mr. and Mrs. Nicholas Jude Strickland

request the honour of your presence

at a ceremony to celebrate

the reaffirmation of their wedding vows

Saturday, the twenty-third of August

at six o'clock

Church of Christ

Bedford, New York

and at a reception afterwards

Sleepy Hollow Country Club

Scarborough

My father became ill a couple of months before I was supposed to be married. Instead of the large church ceremony that we planned, my fiancé and I were married in my father's hospital room. We would still like to be married in our church. How should our invitations read?

Your invitations may be issued by either your mother or by you and your fiancé. If you were married in a religious ceremony, your invitations would read as a reaffirmation of your wedding vows. If, however, you were married in a civil ceremony and now wish to get married in a religious ceremony, your invitations would state that the ceremony was being performed to solemnize your marriage. (To solemnize means to make right before God.)

Mrs. Andrew Jay Forrester

requests the honour of your presence

at the religious ceremony to solemnize

the marriage of her daughter

Jennifer Marie

and

Mr. Nicholas Jude Strickland

etc.

Commitment Ceremonies

A relatively recent cultural development, same-sex unions are not held to the same etiquette standards as traditional weddings. Typically hosted by the couple or one or both sets of parents, the ceremony can be as formal or informal as the couple wishes. Some couples choose to have an officiant at their service while others prefer to have their own words, as well as those of friends and family, serve as the public proclamation of their commitment.

Invitation wording and styles can be just as unique as the ceremony. As with a traditional invitation, the most important thing is that it informs your guests of the date, time, location, and nature of the event. Other than that, each couple is free to choose the design, format, and elements that work for them.

BETHANY AND ELIZABETH

February 7, 2009

Mr. and Mrs. Thomas Alber
request the honour of your presence
at the commitment ceremony of their daughter

BETHANY LYNN ALBER

to

MS. ELIZABETH HARRISON WILKINS

February 13, 2010 at two o'clock in the afternoon

Arlington Chu

▲ Samples of invitations to commitment ceremonies

TOGETHER WITH THEIR FAMILIES

TOM KLEIN AND JAKE CLAIBORNE

INVITE YOU TO SHARE IN THE JOYOUS BEGINNING
OF THEIR NEW LIFE TOGETHER

THE CELEBRATION OF THEIR COMMITMENT AND LOVE
WILL BE HELD ON
SATURDAY, THE FIFTH OF JUNE
TWO THOUSAND TEN
AT SIX O'CLOCK IN THE EVENING
TOM NEVERS BEACH
NANTUCKET, MASSACHUSETTS

INVITATION ENCLOSURES

Reception Cards

Reception cards are used whenever the wedding ceremony and reception are held in different places. Because they are at different locations, they are considered separate events, each requiring their own invitation. Reception cards are not necessary when the ceremony and the reception are held at the same place.

An accompanying reply card allows your guests to notify you if they will or will not be able to attend the wedding and reception.

Composing a Reception Card

The first line on the reception card indicates the occasion. It reads "Breakfast" when occurring before one o'clock (regardless of the menu) and "Reception" when held at one o'clock or later.

The next line indicates the time and usually reads, "immediately following the ceremony." This phrase should not be taken literally as it simply means that the reception will start in, more or less, the amount of time it takes to get from the ceremony to the reception. If the reception is scheduled to start two or more hours after the ceremony ends, the phrase "immediately following the ceremony" should be replaced with the appropriate time. The line may then read, "at eight o'clock."

The name of the facility at which the reception will take place is given on the third line. The address is usually shown on the fourth line, although it is omitted whenever the facility is very well known or when directions and map cards are used.

The city and state follow on the next line if they are not the same as those shown on the invitation. If the city and state do not appear on the reception card, it is assumed that the reception is in the same town as the wedding. Likewise, if the city is different but the state is the same, you need only mention the city. These are options. You may, however, under any circumstances use both city and state.

Responses to Reception Cards

Historically, all social invitations were responded to through a handwritten note. However, over time this particular point of etiquette seemed to fade from the public consciousness and led to the development of reply cards. Most wedding invitation ensembles now include a reply card that serves as a response device for both the wedding and reception.

When reply cards are not being sent, a reply is requested in the lower left-hand corner of the reception card. Corner lines appear in a smaller size than the body of the reception card.

The top line asks your guests to reply by stating either, "The favour of a reply is requested," "R.s.v.p.," or "R.S.V.P." All three are considered proper. However, in some regions, such as the southern United States, "The favour of a reply is requested" is preferred while "R.s.v.p." is frowned upon.

The address to which the replies are to be sent is shown on the following two lines. The address shown is the address of the person whose name first appears on the wedding invitation. So if the invitation was issued by your parents, the lines would contain your parents' address. If you would like to have the replies sent to you, you must put your name, preceded by your title, on the lines beneath the reply request.

Whether you use your address or your parents' address, you should always include an address on your reception cards to reply to even when the same address appears on the invitation's outside envelope (except when also sending reply cards). People tend to discard envelopes, especially when there is an additional inside envelope. If some of your guests throw out their envelopes and there is no address inside, they may not be able to reply. This could result in your having to make some unnecessary phone calls.

Reception
immediately following the ceremony
Sleepy Hollow Country Club
Scarborough, New York

The favour of a reply is requested
2830 Meadowbrook Drive
Bedford, New York 10506

What is the correct spelling of "favor"?

Both "favor" and "favour" are correct. Like "honor" and honour," it is a matter of personal preference, although the vast majority of brides prefer the English spelling, "favour." If you use the English spelling of "honour," use the English spelling of "favour" also, for consistency.

My wedding reception will include a sit-down dinner. How is that indicated?

In most cases, no special designation is made. Many brides, however, worry that their guests might not know that a meal will be served and will make other plans for dinner. You may alert your guests about the dinner by including "Dinner Reception" on the top line of your reception cards.

How do I let my guests know that there will be dancing at the reception?

While some brides use "Dinner and Dancing" on the first line of their reception cards, it is usually not necessary to do so. If there is a band and a dance floor, people will dance.

Although we love our nieces and nephews, we would rather not have any children at our wedding. How can we nicely tell our guests that their children are not invited?

The names of the family members that you are inviting are written on the inside envelope. If children are not invited to your wedding, their names are simply left off the inside envelope. Thus, when "Mr. and Mrs. Sterling" is written on the outside envelope, it means only that Mr. and Mrs. Sterling are invited. If their children were to be invited, the inside envelope would read:

Mr. and Mrs. Sterling
Kathryn, Robby, and John

Of course most people are not familiar with this point of etiquette and a corner line reading, "No children, please" seems a bit cruel, so what else can you do? The best solution is to talk to your family members and friends with children and let them know that, although you would really love to invite their children, expenses (or whatever) prevent you from doing so. A possible compromise might be to invite children to the ceremony but not to the reception. This, too, is best handled by talking it over with those involved.

We are having a formal reception. Where do the words "Black tie" appear?

The time of day actually dictates the formality of dress for the wedding and reception. (After six o'clock is considered formal.) Although some people are familiar with this point of etiquette, most are not. Therefore, you may wish to include "Black tie" on your reception cards to ensure that all of your guests know how to dress.

When using "Black tie," the B is uppercase and the t is lowercase. "Black tie" generally appears in the lower right-hand corner of the reception card. It does not appear on the invitation to the ceremony since it is the reception, not the ceremony, that is formal. When no reception card is used, "Black tie" appears in the lower right-hand corner of the invitation. If you do not like corner lines on invitations, you may include a reception card to indicate the type of dress.

What does "White tie" signify?

White-tie events are even more formal than black-tie events. They require men to wear white tie, wing collar, and tailcoat. Women wear evening gowns.

What does "Black tie optional" mean?

While "Black tie optional" is sometimes used, it is not correct and may cause confusion since it literally means that you may dress any way you please, with a tuxedo being one of the acceptable choices. If you want to be assured that all your guests wear formal attire, you'll want to drop the "optional" from your wording.

What does "R.s.v.p." stand for?

"R.s.v.p." is French for "Répondez s'il vous plaît." Its use on an invitation requires a response.

My reception is being held at my parents' house. How are my reception cards worded?

If your parents are hosting your wedding and their names are on the first line of the wedding invitations, the location lines on the reception cards show their home address. Your guests will know that it is their address because no other names are mentioned. When reply cards are not sent, the corner line on the reception card reads "The favour of a reply is requested," "R.s.v.p," or "R.S.V.P." Your parents' address is not shown beneath the reply request since it has already been given in the body of the reception card.

My reception is being held at a friend's house. How is that worded?

When a reception is held at the home of a friend, your friend's name and address are given on the location lines. A line reading, "at the residence of" precedes his or her name and address.

Reception

immediately following the ceremony

at the residence of

Mr. and Mrs. Michael Anthony LaPointe

211 Old Orchard Road

Bedford

My fiancé and I are saving our money to buy a house. Therefore, we would rather receive cash than gifts. How do we let our guests know this?

While an occasional bride and groom establish a money tree and ask their guests to contribute toward it, in some circles it is still considered incorrect and in very poor taste to ask your guests for money. First of all, it is presumptuous on your part to expect a gift from everybody to whom invitations are sent. Second, a number of your guests will probably want to give you a special gift to be remembered by. Asking for money directly is much too mercenary. (Of course, there is no reason why your parents, when asked, could not suggest a check.)

Our wedding is being held in a church and our reception will be at my parents' country club. Where on the invitations does the reception information appear?

Weddings and receptions held at separate locations are considered separate events and require separate invitations. Reception cards serve as invitations to the reception and are used whenever the wedding and the reception are held in different locations. In the case of a formal wedding, the reception information should not appear on the wedding invitation itself.

If you are doing a less formal wedding invitation and wanted to combine the wedding and the reception information on one invitation, you could add a couple of lines to the invitation beneath the city and state that read, "and afterwards at the reception / Sleepy Hollow Country Club," "and afterward at the reception / Sleepy Hollow Country Club / Scarborough," or "Reception to follow / Sleepy Hollow Country Club / Scarborough."

Is it proper to have guests respond by phone, fax, or email?

Social invitations should be responded to in writing. This includes the completion and return of an enclosed reply card. The use of a telephone, fax, or email for responses is reserved for business and informal social occasions.

How do I let my guests know where I am registered?

It is in very poor taste to include a card announcing the store at which you are registered. That is too much like asking for a gift. The best way to let people know is by word of mouth. If this is not practical, the save-the-date would be the least offensive place to include it. With the evolution of the web, many couples now have wedding home pages. The URL for the pages is often included on their save-the-date card. Registry information is often included on the website.

My reception is going to take place on a yacht. How is that worded?

The wording is similar to that on a standard reception card. The location line reads, "aboard the *Mirabella*" or whatever the name of the yacht is. The next line shows the name of the yacht club or marina out of which it will sail.

How can we make sure that our guests don't miss the boat?

You may add two lines to the lower right-hand corner of your reception cards that read, "The *Mirabella* / sails promptly at eight o'clock."

Reply Cards

In the past, a wedding invitation was properly responded to through a handwritten note. Over time and owing to many factors, including a lack of understanding of social etiquette and increased demands on individual time, this tradition has fallen by the wayside and reply cards have become a standard element in the current wedding invitation sets. (For more on how to prepare a handwritten response, see page 94.)

Reply cards can be produced in a number of different formats. All formats, however, share similar features. Spaces are always provided for the guests' names and for their responses. A request for a response is always included as well, usually before a specific date. The reply request may be made in either the first two lines of the reply card or in the lower left-hand corner. Some brides choose not to include a date in their reply request as they feel it might insult guests who know very well when to reply. The name and address of whoever will receive the replies appear on the face of the reply envelopes.

A Look Back: WOMEN AS SOCIAL SECRETARIES

Historically, women were the social secretaries of their households. Any correspondence that needed to be sent on behalf of the household was handled by the "lady of the house." Since she did not work outside the home (or inside, for that matter, since the "help" performed most of the household tasks), she had plenty of time to serve as social secretary. Among the functions she performed was handwriting responses to invitations. Years ago, all responses to formal wedding invitations were handwritten on plain, unembellished letter sheets.

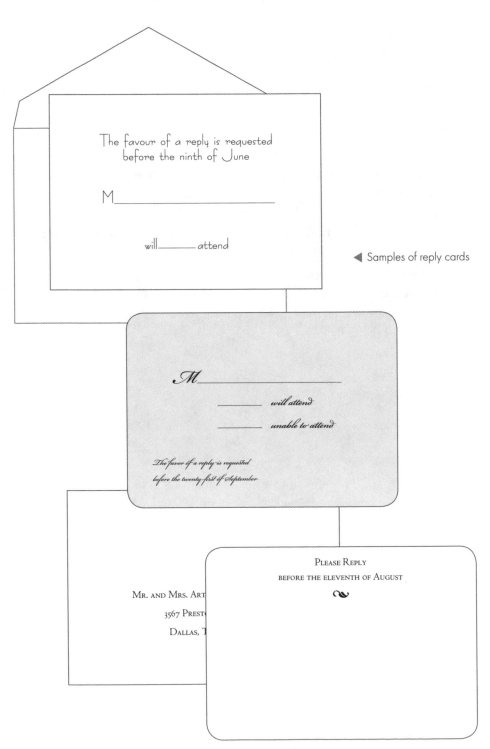

The favour of a reply is requested
before the ninth of June

M_____

will_____attend

◄ Samples of reply cards

*M*_____

_____ *will attend*

_____ *unable to attend*

The favor of a reply is requested
before the twenty-first of September

PLEASE REPLY
BEFORE THE ELEVENTH OF AUGUST

❧

Mr. and Mrs. Art

3567 Prest

Dallas, T

FILLING IN REPLY CARDS

Reply cards are easier to use than they appear to be. A space, usually following an "M," is provided for your titles and names. (The "M" is provided to help you get started with your title, assuming your title begins with an "M." If it does not, you may draw a slash through the "M" and write out "Doctor" or whatever your title may be.) The next line allows you to tell your hosts whether or not you will be attending. If you are, the space is left blank. If you are unable to attend, you write in "not." You then place the card inside its envelope and mail it.

WHAT NAMES ARE USED ON REPLY CARDS?

Your full social names with titles are used. If you are married, your names read, "Mr. and Mrs." followed by your husband's first, middle, and last names.

I RECEIVED A BLANK CARD WITH JUST "THE FAVOUR OF A REPLY IS REQUESTED" ON IT. WHAT SHOULD I DO?

Blank reply cards are sent when a bride would like a formal response but is afraid that if she does not send reply cards, she will not get many responses. Since the bride provided you the card and the opportunity to write a formal response, you should do so. (See page 94 for more information.)

Since my parents, my fiancé, and I are all doctors, many of our guests are also doctors. Should my reply cards be done differently?

Since many of your guests will be doctors, you may wish to omit the "M" on the reply cards. This leaves your reply cards with a blank name line and allows your guests to write in their appropriate titles.

I would like to receive handwritten responses but I'm afraid that if I don't send reply cards, I won't hear from everybody.

One solution is to send reply cards that are blank except for the words "The favour of a reply is requested" across the top or the bottom of the card. A sec-

UPDATED: *Keepsake Reply Cards*

Very often couples like to invite their guests to do more than say "yes" or "no" on the reply card. By printing "The favor of a reply" line near the top of the reply card, you leave room for your guests to write in any special comments or notes regarding your union. Many couples choose to retain cards with handwritten notes as yet another memento of the occasion.

ond possibility is to take a small fold-over note, turn it on its side so that the fold is on the left-hand side, and print. The note becomes a miniature version of the letter sheet that is properly used for handwritten responses.

My family knows how to properly respond to wedding invitations but, unfortunately, my fiancé's family does not. Can I send reply cards to some guests and not to others?

If you are afraid of offending some of your guests by sending them reply cards, you may send reply cards just to those who you feel would need them. This, of course, requires two sets of reception cards: one with the reply request in the lower left-hand corner for those guests not receiving reply cards and another without the reply request for those guests who are receiving reply cards.

What date should be used for the reply request?

Most couples ask that their replies be received two weeks before their wedding date. Caterers, restaurants, clubs, and other locations typically look for a final count five days before the event. When choosing your venue, be sure to ask the manager their timeframe for a specific count.

Our reception will feature a choice of three different meals. The caterer would like to know ahead of time how many of each to prepare. Is it proper to ask for that information on our reply cards?

While once considered inappropriate, it is now not uncommon for meal selections to be included on the reply card. Just be mindful that the reply card is an appropriate size to accommodate the inclusion of additional information requests. A larger size may be necessary to keep the card looking neat and elegant.

Our caterer needs to know how many guests we expect at our wedding. Would it be helpful to put a line requesting "number of guests" on our reply cards?

Although having your guests fill in a space asking how many of them will be attending would definitely help you in obtaining an accurate count, there is one very serious drawback. By doing so, you encourage your guests to bring along more people than you otherwise would have invited. An invitation addressed to "Mr. and Mrs. Smith" with a reply card asking them how many people are coming might lead them to think that not only are they invited but also their kids and, perhaps, their Aunt Sally who, as it happens, will be in town that week. Giving your guests an opportunity like that can be asking for trouble.

Do I need to include a stamp on the reply set envelope?

There are two schools of thought when it comes to pre-stamping the reply envelope. Some people feel quite strongly that guests should feel honored to be invited to the wedding and more than willing to provide a stamp for their response. Others believe that providing a stamp is a matter of common courtesy and given that guests may incur expenses related to travel and lodging around the wedding, it is a small price to pay to make a guest feel welcome.

The best advice is to do what feels right to you. Your guests will no doubt respond no matter which course you choose.

When should responses be sent?

Most invitations mention the date by which responses are needed. Your response should be mailed so that it arrives before its deadline. If no date is mentioned, responses should be sent three days after the invitation is received.

Reply Envelopes

Reply envelopes must always be included when a reply card is provided. The address of the issuer of the wedding invitation, not the bride or groom, should appear on the face of the envelope. While the inclusion of return postage is a matter of choice, most people include it as a courtesy to their guests.

FILLING IN REPLY CARDS

Although most wedding invitations are sent with reply cards, many are sent with a reply request on the reception card instead. These invitations require a handwritten response. Formal responses are handwritten on ecru letter sheets. These sheets were traditionally blank but may now have a tasteful monogram blind-embossed on the top.

Responses follow the format of the invitations. Since wedding invitations are issued in the third person, responses are written in the third person as well. The guests' full social names and titles are used while only the hosts' titles and surnames are written. On the envelopes, however, the hosts' full names are used with their titles. Acceptances repeat the date and time while regrets repeat just the date. There is no need to mention the reason for not attending.

ACCEPTANCE:

Mr. and Mrs. Edward Allen Singer
accept with pleasure
the kind invitation of
Mr. and Mrs. Forrester
for Saturday, the twenty-third of August
at six o'clock

REGRET:

Mr. and Mrs. Edward Allen Singer
regret that they are unable to accept
the kind invitation of
Mr. and Mrs. Forrester
for Saturday, the twenty-third of August

IN WHAT COLOR INK SHOULD RESPONSES BE WRITTEN?

Formal responses may be written in blue or black ink. Most people, however, prefer black ink since it usually matches the invitations.

HOW IS THE RESPONSE WRITTEN WHEN CHILDREN ARE INVITED?

The names used in your response should be the same as those written on the inside envelope you received. If your children are invited, their names will be listed on the face of the inside envelope, beneath yours. When writing your response, repeat the names as they are written on the inside envelope.

Mr. and Mrs. Edward Allen Singer
Esta, Janice, and Barbara
accept with pleasure

etc.

MY HUSBAND AND I WERE BOTH INVITED TO MY COUSIN'S WEDDING. I WILL BE ABLE TO GO BUT MY HUSBAND WILL BE OUT OF TOWN. HOW SHOULD MY RESPONSE READ?

Your response begins with a formal acceptance on your part. Your husband's regret is added at the end.

Mrs. Edward Allen Singer
accepts with pleasure
the kind invitation of
Mr. and Mrs. Forrester
for Saturday, the twenty-third of August
at six o'clock
Mr. Edward Allen Singer
regrets that he is unable to attend

At-Home Cards

Family and friends can be made aware of your new address when at-home cards are included with your invitations and announcements. At-home cards are small enclosure cards whose card stock, lettering style, and ink color match the invita-

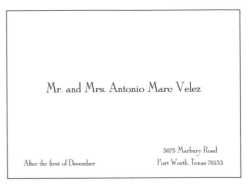

Mr. and Mrs. Antonio Marc Velez

After the first of December

3675 Marbury Road
Fort Worth, Texas 76133

▲ Sample of an at-home card

tions with which they are sent. They alert people of the address at which you will be residing and the date after which you will be there. Many couples now include their phone numbers and email addresses on their at-home cards.

The wording for at-home cards sent with announcements is different from the wording for at-home cards sent with the invitations. At-home cards sent with announcements show your names together as "Mr. and Mrs." since you are already married when they are sent. When sent with invitations your names are not used since you are not yet married and cannot use "Mr. and Mrs."

While the principal purpose of at-home cards is to let people know your new address, when sent with announcements they can also let people know that you have chosen to continue using your maiden name. Your name appears on the first line followed by your husband's name on line two. The remainder of the card reads as it normally would. Since you could have presented yourself as "Mrs." but did not, it will be assumed that you are still using your maiden name.

ROOTED IN TRADITION: *Home, first Home*
The tradition of at-home cards dates back to a time when the bride and groom returned from their honeymoon to their first home together.

I would like to send at–home cards with my wedding announcements but I don't want anybody to think that I'm asking for gifts.

At-home cards are like the change-of-address cards you might send when you move. They simply announce your new address and are a great convenience for anyone who wants to keep in touch with you. They are not gift-request cards and should never be interpreted as such.

What date should we use on our at–home cards?

Most couples use the date on which they return from their honeymoon.

Direction and Map Cards

Out-of-town guests will appreciate receiving direction cards or map cards. Direction cards give simple yet explicit directions to your wedding, while map cards are maps with the routes to your wedding highlighted. Map cards generally feature major roads and landmarks to help your guests find their way. When direction cards or map cards are included, the street address does not appear on the invitations.

As with other enclosures, direction cards and map cards should complement the wedding invitations. They typically match the invitation style and color. To make them easier to read, a sans serif (block) lettering style is usually used.

Direction cards and map cards are usually sent with the wedding invitations but may be sent afterwards in an envelope or as a postcard to those who accept your invitation. When sent afterwards, a line reading, "We are looking forward to having you attend" may be added to the top of the cards.

Ceremony Cards

For large receptions with small, private ceremonies, invitations are sent to the reception. Guests invited to the ceremony are sent smaller ceremony cards enclosed with their reception invitations. The same size as reception cards, ceremony cards serve as invitations to the ceremony. They are usually designed to match the reception invitation but they may be handwritten when the guest list is small.

The wording "Request the honour of your presence" is used when the ceremony is held in a church while "request the pleasure of your company" is used when it is held elsewhere. Both "marriage ceremony" and "wedding ceremony" are proper. Whichever word ("marriage" or "wedding") is used on the reception invitations must be repeated on the ceremony card.

Accommodation Cards

Accommodation cards are enclosed with the invitations sent to out-of-town guests who are unfamiliar with the area and need to make hotel reservations. They list the names and phone numbers of nearby hotels. If you are paying for your guests' rooms, a notation to that effect is made on the cards.

Within-the-Ribbon Cards

Pews may be cordoned off with white ribbons or cords to indicate a special seating section. When this is done, small cards reading "Within the ribbon" are sent with the invitations to those guests who will be seated in that section. The guests then bring the cards to the ceremony, which enables the ushers to seat them in the appropriate section.

Pew Cards

Pew cards are used when specific pews have been assigned for some or all of the guests. This helps the ushers efficiently guide their guests to their assigned seats. Pew cards are sent with the invitations. A space on the card is filled in by hand with the appropriate pew.

Admission Cards

Admission cards are a lot like tickets to the theater or to a ball game—you need to present them to gain admittance. Admission cards are generally used by well-known people who want to make sure that only invited guests are allowed to attend their wedding. They are sent with the invitations to all guests and may be personalized.

Transportation Cards

When a large number of out-of-town guests are attending a wedding, especially one in a big city, transportation from the wedding to the reception is occasionally provided. Sent with the invitations, transportation cards let your guests know that their local travel plans have been taken care of. The cards generally read, "Transportation will be provided / from the ceremony to the reception."

◀ Sample of a direction card

*From the Cincinnatian Hotel
to Ault Park Pavilion*

TURN ONTO VINE STREET, THEN RIGHT ONTO US-22.
TAKE RAMP ONTO I-71 NORTH.
AT EXIT 6, TURN RIGHT ONTO SR-561 (EDWARDS ROAD).
TURN LEFT ONTO OBSERVATORY AVENUE.
FOLLOW SIGNS TO THE PAVILION.

*From Ault Park Pavilion
to Maketewah Country Club*

EXIT THE PARK ON OBSERVATORY AVENUE.
TURN RIGHT ONTO SR-561 (EDWARDS ROAD).
TAKE RAMP ONTO I-71 NORTH.
AT EXIT 7, TURN RIGHT ONTO SR-562.
TURN RIGHT ON US-42 (READING ROAD).
THE COUNTRY CLUB IS LE
AT 5401 READING ROAD.

The honour of your presence is requested

at the marriage ceremony

Friday evening, the fifth of October

at six o'clock

First Presbyterian Church

Philadelphia

▲ Sample of a
ceremony card

Please present this card

at All Saints' Episcopal Church

Saturday, the fifteenth of September

Pew number _____

▲ Sample of a pew card

PREPARING YOUR INVITATION FOR MAILING

Addressing the Envelopes

Wedding invitations were once delivered by hand. If you were a bride back in those days, your footman delivered your invitations to your guests' homes. Their servants received the invitations and removed them from their outer envelope, an envelope much too pedestrian for your guests to handle themselves. The servants, then, presented the invitation to your guests in its pristine inside envelope. Because the invitations were already at their destination, the inside envelopes had only the names of your guests written on them. The address was no longer needed. They just had to be directed to the appropriate members of the household.

Following tradition, wedding invitations are still sometimes sent in two envelopes. The outside envelope is the mailing envelope. Your guests' names and addresses are written on its face. No abbreviations are used in the address. "Rural Route" and "Post Office Box" are always written out.

Your guests' names are repeated on the inside envelope. This time, however, only their titles and surnames are used. If children under the age of eighteen are invited, their first names would appear on the line beneath their parents' names.

The back flap of the outside envelope bears the sender's address.

While you may use any color ink you please to address your envelopes, you want to be certain the handwriting is neat and legible. Many couples choose to retain a calligrapher to address their invitations. If a calligrapher is not a viable alternative and your handwriting is not the best, you may consider running the envelopes through your computer printer. There are a number of suitably elegant typefaces for the job.

One word of caution, with some printers, the inside envelope, which is often on a heavier stock than the outside envelope and lined, will prove too thick to run through the printer. Because the style of lettering on the inside and outside envelopes needs to match, this technical challenge may eliminate this option for you.

Only the address appears on the envelope flap. The names do not. The apartment number must be given when applicable, since without the name there would be no way of identifying the sender. The apartment may appear alone on the first line with "Apartment" spelled out or at the

ROOTED IN TRADITION: *The Flap Over the Flap*

Traditionally the address was blind-embossed or engraved on the envelope flap. Blind-embossing is the more traditional of the two and was preferred over engraving because of the feeling that the first time guests see engraving, it should be on the invitations. The return address, on the other hand, should melt into the background.

end of the street address, preceded by a comma or a bullet. (A bullet is a period that is raised to a point halfway between the top and bottom of a line.)

The address of whoever issued the invitations appears on the back flap. If, for example, your parents issued your invitations, their address appears. Many people, however, use the return address as an indication where the gifts should be sent, so if you would like to have your presents sent directly to you, you may use your address for the return address.

We are sending wedding invitations to two sisters who are living together. Whose name is first?

When addressing envelopes to two or more siblings under the age of eighteen who are living at home, the name of the oldest child is listed first followed by the names of his or her siblings in reverse chronological order. If they are over eighteen, they receive separate invitations.

We are sending wedding invitations to a couple with two children. Do we use "and family" on the outside envelope?

No. Wedding invitations are sent to the adult members of the household. In your case, the outside envelope is addressed to the parents who receive the invitations on behalf of their children. Their children's names (not "and family"), if you wish to invite them, are written on the inside envelope on a line beneath the names of their parents. (See page 85 for more on inviting older children.)

Addressing the Envelopes

	OUTSIDE ENVELOPE	INSIDE ENVELOPE
MARRIED COUPLE	Mr. and Mrs. Troy Clayton	Mr. and Mrs. Clayton
WITH CHILDREN UNDER EIGHTEEN LIVING AT HOME*	Mr. and Mrs. Troy Clayton	Mr. and Mrs. Clayton Marvin and Heather

* The name of the oldest child is listed first followed by the names of his or her siblings in reverse chronological order.

	OUTSIDE ENVELOPE	INSIDE ENVELOPE
WITH CHILDREN OVER EIGHTEEN LIVING AT HOME*	Miss Heather Clayton OR Mr. Marvin Clayton	Miss Clayton OR Mr. Clayton

* Children over the age of eighteen should each receive a separate invitation.

	OUTSIDE ENVELOPE	INSIDE ENVELOPE
IN WHICH WOMAN KEPT MAIDEN NAME	Ms. Christine Pritchett and Mr. Troy Clayton	Ms. Pritchett and Mr. Clayton
IN WHICH MAN IS A DOCTOR	Doctor and Mrs. Troy Clayton	Doctor and Mrs. Clayton
IN WHICH BOTH ARE DOCTORS	The Doctors Clayton OR Doctor Christine Clayton and Doctor Troy Clayton OR Doctor and Mrs. Troy Clayton	The Doctors Clayton OR Doctor and Mrs. Clayton

	OUTSIDE ENVELOPE	INSIDE ENVELOPE
IN WHICH WOMAN IS A DOCTOR	Mr. and Mrs. Troy Clayton OR Doctor Christine Clayton and Mr. Troy Clayton	Doctor Clayton and Mr. Clayton OR Mr. and Mrs. Clayton
IN WHICH MAN IS A JUDGE	The Honorable and Mrs. Troy Clayton	Judge and Mrs. Clayton
IN WHICH THE WOMAN IS A JUDGE	Mr. and Mrs. Troy Clayton OR The Honorable Christine Clayton and Mr. Troy Clayton	Mr. and Mrs. Clayton OR Judge Clayton and Mr. Clayton
IN WHICH BOTH ARE LAWYERS	Mr. and Mrs. Troy Clayton	Mr. and Mrs. Clayton
UNMARRIED COUPLE LIVING TOGETHER	Miss Christine Pritchett Mr. Troy Clayton OR Ms. Christine Pritchett Mr. Troy Clayton	Miss Pritchett Mr. Clayton OR Ms. Pritchett Mr. Clayton

We are sending invitations to a "junior." Do we use "junior"?

If "junior" is a part of a man's name, you would include it (or "Jr.") on the outside envelope. It is not necessary to repeat it on the inside envelope unless both "junior" and "senior" are living at the same address.

Should we use numerals or should we write out the numbers?

Numerals are usually used for the street number, although it is also appropriate to write out numbers one through twenty. Numbered streets may appear whichever way is more aesthetically pleasing. Numerals are always used for zip codes.

How can I tell which envelopes are the mailing envelopes?

It is easy to tell which envelopes are which. The outside envelopes have glue on them; the inside envelopes do not and they are also a bit smaller. To avoid confusion when addressing envelopes, it is best to work with one set of envelopes at a time. Address all the outside envelopes first. After those are all addressed, start addressing the inside envelopes. That will make it almost impossible to address the wrong envelopes.

I am addressing an envelope to a man and a woman who are living together. Whose name goes first?

The woman's name should appear on the first line and the man's on the second.

A number of our friends are seeing somebody. We would like to invite them to our wedding. How is that done?

The nicest way to invite dates is to call your friends, get the names of their dates, and send them each an invitation. A less formal way is to address the inside envelopes with either "Mr. Clayton and guest" or "Miss Clayton and escort." Women who feel that an escort is unnecessary in this day and age prefer "Miss Clayton and guest" or "Ms. Clayton and guest."

Assembling the Invitation

Your wedding invitations may arrive already stuffed into their inner envelopes or in separate stacks of invitations, enclosure cards, and inner and outer envelopes. If yours come unassembled, there is no need to panic. Assembling wedding invitations is really quite simple, albeit time consuming.

UPDATED: *Personalized Stamps*

Thanks to modern technology, even your postage stamp can be customized to match your wedding invitation. Working with the U.S. Postal Service or other online services, you can upload images, including motifs from your invitation or photos, to bring a personal touch to the outside of your invitation envelope. Customized stamps are also a popular choice for save-the-date cards and thank-you notes.

For the most part, wedding invitations are assembled in size order. The invitation itself is first. The enclosure cards are stacked on top of the invitations, not inside. The reception card is placed on top of the invitation. Then the reply envelope is placed face down on the reception card. The reply card is slipped face up beneath the flap of the reply envelope. These are the most frequently used enclosures. Any other enclosures are added face up in size order (usually at-home card, direction card, accommodation card, pew card, etc.).

The single-fold invitation and its enclosures are placed into the inside envelope with the fold of the invitation at the bottom of the envelope and the engraving facing the back of the envelope. You can tell whether or not you stuffed the envelope correctly by removing the invitation with your right hand. If you can read the invitation without turning it, it was stuffed correctly.

The procedure for assembling traditional invitations (those with a second fold) is similar. The enclosures are placed on top of the lower half of the invitation's face in the same order described above. The invitation is folded from top to bottom over the enclosures. The invitation is then placed into the inside envelope with the fold toward the bottom of the envelope. As with other invitations, traditional invitations are correctly stuffed when they can be read without being turned, after being removed from the envelope with your right hand.

Once stuffed, the inside envelopes are inserted into the outside envelopes. The front of the inside envelope faces the back of the outside envelope.

My invitations came with tissues. Should I send them or remove them?

All wedding invitations were once shipped with small pieces of tissue separating each invitation. This prevented the slow-drying ink from smudging. Before mailing her invitations, the bride removed the tissues, as they were merely packing material and served no point of etiquette. Through the years, many brides, unaware of the impropriety of sending tissued invitations, left the tissues in. As this practice grew, tissued invitations became as proper as nontissued invitations.

Today, wedding invitations are properly sent both ways. Tissues are starting to serve an important function again as the postal service's sorting equipment can cause smudging on invitations sent without tissues. If you are sending invitations without tissues, you may be able to ask your local post office to hand-cancel them. Hand-canceling also prevents the postal service from printing their advertising, disguised as part of the cancellation mark, on your wedding invitations.

Where are the tissues placed?

Since the tissues are meant to prevent smudging, they should be placed over the copy on each invitation and enclosure.

Mailing Your Invitation

When should my wedding invitations be mailed?

Wedding invitations should be mailed four to six weeks before the wedding. For summer and holiday weddings, many brides mail their invitations eight weeks before the wedding since people are more likely to be traveling at those times.

How much postage will my wedding invitations require?

The invitation's size and the number of enclosure cards affect the postage. To determine the correct postage, you should have your invitations (including

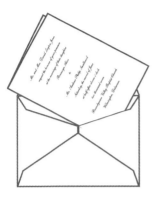

▲ A single-fold invitation
inserted into an envelope

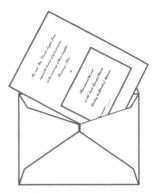

▲ Inserting a single-fold invitation
with an enclosure card

▲ A two-fold invitation
inserted into an envelope

▲ Inserting a two-fold invitation
with an enclosure card

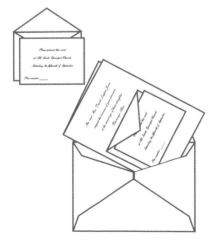

▲ Enclosing a reply card
and envelope

▲ Placing an inner envelope
into an outer envelope

the stamp on the reply envelope) weighed at the post office from which they will be sent.

How much money should I expect to spend?

Costs will vary as they are determined by the quality of the invitation, the printing method used to produce them, the number of enclosures, and the quantity ordered. When selecting your invitations, it is important to remember that even though the invitations set the tone for the entire wedding, they comprise, on average, only about 2 percent of the cost of the wedding. No matter how much money you save by purchasing inexpensive invitations, it will be a tiny amount in relation to the overall cost of your wedding.

RECEPTION INVITATIONS

Invitations to the Reception

On occasion a couple may choose to have a small, intimate wedding ceremony with only the closest of family and friends in attendance, followed by a larger reception. Since more people are invited to the reception than the ceremony, the invitations are for the reception.

Reception invitations always "request the pleasure of your company" since the reception is not being held in a house of worship. The word "and" is used to join the names of the bride and groom. The phrases "marriage reception" and "wedding reception" are both correct. "Marriage reception" is the more traditional of the two but many couples prefer "wedding reception," arguing that a wedding is the act of getting married while marriage is the result of that decision.

The same rules regarding the sequence of wording, use of social titles, addressing the envelopes, etc. that apply to wedding invitations also apply to reception invitations.

An invitation to a reception is also sent to those guests who will be attending the ceremony. The invitation to the ceremony is either extended orally or through a ceremony card included with the reception invitation. If a ceremony card is used, it is important that the wording of the card matches that of the reception card. (For more on ceremony cards see page 97.)

RECEPTION INVITATION:

Mr. and Mrs. Andrew Jay Forrester

request the pleasure of your company

at the marriage reception of their daughter

Jennifer Marie

and

Mr. Nicholas Jude Strickland

Saturday, the twenty-third of August

at seven o'clock

Sleepy Hollow Country Club

Scarborough, New York

CEREMONY CARD:

The honour of your presence is requested

at the marriage ceremony

Saturday, the twenty-third of August

at six o'clock

Church of Christ

Bedford

Late Receptions

Wedding receptions take place on the day of the wedding. Any reception occurring after that date is not properly referred to as a wedding reception. Rather, it is a party or reception in honor of the recently married couple.

These types of receptions are held for a variety of reasons. Most late receptions are held when the bride and her family live in different parts of the country. Others, especially those involving older couples or second-time brides, may hold late receptions due to professional considerations. Whatever the reasons, late receptions are becoming a more common occurrence.

The wording for invitations to a late reception should contain a line reading "in honour of" or "in honor of" followed on a separate line with the names of the couple.

We are having a small ceremony for just our families in August. We are also planning a reception in September. Is it proper to send our reception invitations with our wedding announcements?

Reception invitations are never properly sent with announcements. Your wedding and your late reception are separate events that require separate mailings.

We are having a small reception immediately following our wedding and a larger reception a month later. May we enclose a reception card for our late reception?

Receptions that take place after the wedding day are not considered wedding receptions. They are simply parties in honor of the couple. The party is an event that is not a part of your wedding, so it requires separate invitations and a separate mailing.

Mr. and Mrs. Andrew Jay Forrester

request the pleasure of your company

at the dinner reception

in the honour of

Mr. and Mrs. Nicholas Jude Strickland

Saturday, the twentieth of September

at seven o'clock

Sleepy Hollow Country Club

Scarborough, New York

REVISING AN ISSUED ANNOUNCEMENT OR INVITATION

Postponement of a Wedding

Weddings are occasionally postponed due to illness or an unexpected death in the family. If you have not yet mailed your invitations, you may include a small card informing your guests of the new date. If your invitation has already been mailed, an announcement should be prepared and mailed immediately. If time does not permit for printing and mailing in a timely manner (i.e. to arrive at least two weeks before the wedding), your guests may be notified of the new date by phone.

POSTPONEMENT ANNOUNCEMENT:

Mr. and Mrs. Andrew Jay Forrester

announce that the marriage of their daughter

Jennifer Marie

to

Mr. Nicholas Jude Strickland

has been postponed to

Saturday, the twentieth of September

at six o'clock

Church of Christ

Bedford, New York

Recalling Wedding Invitations

Wedding invitations are recalled when a wedding needs to be postponed before a new wedding date has been set. Recalling invitations officially cancels them so new invitations must be reissued to invite your guests once a new date has been set.

The reason that the invitations are being recalled is usually mentioned. If there is not enough time to send recall notices so that your guests may change their plans without great inconvenience or cost, you may notify them by phone.

RECALL NOTICE:

Mr. and Mrs. Andrew Jay Forrester

regret that the illness of their daughter

Jennifer Marie

obliges them to recall their invitations

to her marriage to

Mr. Nicholas Jude Strickland

on Saturday, the twenty-third of September

NEW INVITATION:

Mr. and Mrs. Andrew Jay Forrester

announce that the wedding of their daughter

Jennifer Marie

to

Mr. Nicholas Jude Strickland

which was postponed, will now take place

on Saturday, the twenty-third of October

etc.

Canceling a Wedding

When a wedding needs to be canceled, formal announcements may be sent. If there is not enough time to send a formal announcement, phone calls may be made instead.

WEDDING CANCELLATION:

Mr. and Mrs. Andrew Jay Forrester

are obliged to recall their invitation

to the marriage of their daughter

Jennifer Marie

to

Mr. Nicholas Jude Strickland

as the marriage will not take place

CHAPTER THREE

For the Groom and His Family

*W*hile the bride's family is traditionally responsible for issuing the bulk of the correspondence surrounding the wedding, the groom and his family also have their roles and responsibilities. As the groom's family would like to be informed and included in any decisions relating to their son's wedding, they should also advise the bride's family before issuing any invitations or announcements related to the wedding.

INVITATIONS TO AN ENGAGEMENT PARTY

Engagement parties are often hosted by the bride's parents but it is perfectly acceptable for any other family member or friend to host one. If it is more practical for the groom's parents to host a party, they may do so instead. The party itself may be as simple as a cocktail party or brunch or as formal as a sit-down meal at their home or at a restaurant. The invitations should say that the event is being held in honor of the couple, although they do not usually mention that it is in honor of the engagement. The guests will undoubtedly figure out the purpose of the event on their own.

Mr. and Mrs. Andrew Jay Forrester

request the pleasure of your company

at a dinner in honour of

Miss Jennifer Marie Forrester

and Mr. Nicholas Jude Strickland

Friday, the thirtieth of March

at seven o'clock

2830 Meadowbrook Drive

Bedford, New York

Our engagement will be announced at the party. How should the invitation read?

If your engagement is being announced at an engagement party, neither your name nor your fiancé's should appear on the invitation, as that would likely give away the surprise. The invitations read as though they are not for any special event other than to enjoy the company of family and good friends.

Two of my parents' closest friends have offered to host my engagement party. How should the invitation read?

When an engagement party is hosted by friends of your parents, the invitations are issued by your parents' friends so their names appear on the first line of the invitation. Your parents' names are not mentioned.

INVITATIONS TO MEET YOU OR YOUR FIANCÉE

In lieu of an engagement party or in addition to an engagement party hosted by the bride's parents, a party to meet you or your fiancée may be in order. If, for example, the bride's parents held an engagement party in New York and your parents in California want to host a party as well, they may host a party "to meet" the bride. This party gives your family and friends an opportunity to get to know the bride before the wedding. The party is in the bride's honor and the invitations should allude to that.

To meet

Miss Jennifer Marie Forrester

Mr. and Mrs. John Peter Strickland

request the pleasure of your company

at a cocktail reception

Friday, the sixth of March

at eight o'clock

910 Oakland Drive

San Marino, California

WEDDING INVITATIONS ISSUED BY THE GROOM'S PARENTS

On rare occasions, perhaps when the bride's parents are deceased or when they live in a foreign country, the groom's parents may issue the wedding invitations. The format is a little different from the standard format. The parents' relationship to the groom is mentioned on the fifth line of the invitation instead of on the third line. This way, the invitations can still be read as the bride being married to the groom. Both the bride and the groom use their full names, preceded by their titles.

Mr. and Mrs. John Peter Strickland

request the pleasure of your company

at the marriage of

Miss Jennifer Marie Forrester

to their son

Mr. Nicholas Jude Strickland

etc.

REHEARSAL DINNER INVITATIONS

Custom suggests that the groom's parents host the rehearsal dinner and, therefore, issue its invitations. The rehearsal dinner takes place on the night before the wedding and is given as a courtesy to the bride's family. The rehearsal dinner invitations are usually worded formally, but many times just first names are used. This less formal style can be a way to let guests know how you, your fiancée, and your fiancée's parents wish to be addressed.

Mr. and Mrs. John Peter Strickland

request the pleasure of your company

at the rehearsal dinner

in honour of

Miss Jennifer Marie Forrester

and

Mr. Nicholas Jude Strickland

Friday, the twenty-second of August

at half after seven o'clock

Tappan Hill

Tarrytown, New York

Nellie and John Strickland

request the pleasure of your company

at the rehearsal dinner for

jen & nick

Friday, August 22nd

at 7:30pm

Tappan Hill

Tarrytown, New York

▲ Sample rehearsal dinner invitations

While invitations to the rehearsal dinner should reflect the nature of the event, they should not compete with or upstage the wedding invitation.

Who is invited to the rehearsal dinner?

Traditionally, the rehearsal dinner was held for just the wedding party in order to get them fed after the rehearsal—and to give the bride's mother one less responsibility. While many rehearsal dinners are still reserved for the wedding party, others have expanded to include the wedding party, their spouses or dates, and out-of-town guests.

When are rehearsal dinner invitations sent?

The invitations are sent two weeks before the wedding.

Very few people are being invited to our rehearsal dinner. Do we need engraved invitations?

Traditional, engraved invitations are rarely used for rehearsal dinners any more. There are other printing options, such as thermography, that produce an attractive, formal invitation at a much more reasonable cost.

CHAPTER FOUR

At the Wedding

A relatively new addition to the wedding celebration, a well-thought-out program can truly enhance your guests' enjoyment of the ceremony. By providing a specific chronology of the rites and events that will take place during your ceremony, as well as listing the names of the bridal party, officiants, and any other participants, a wedding program allows your guests to follow along and makes them feel more included in the entire celebration.

Do I need to have a wedding program?

While there are no hard and fast rules on having a program, in certain circumstances they are almost essential.

If you are having a ceremony with religious or cultural traditions that many of your guests may not be familiar with, you may want to consider having one. Information in the program will help them better grasp the significance and meaning of any rites or traditions you are incorporating.

Programs are also helpful if you have a large wedding where the guests may not be familiar with the members of the bridal party.

Many couples also choose to use the program to formally and publicly thank people who have been helpful and supportive to them in their lives and to pay tribute to a deceased loved one.

DESIGNING YOUR WEDDING PROGRAM

The design of your wedding program should complement your invitation but not necessarily match it. The program should inform your guests of the order of events for the ceremony, who the participants are, and any other special notes regarding the reception or other wedding-related information. Do not sacrifice any of these elements in order to include a graphic or motif on your invitation.

A CELEBRATION OF MARRIAGE

Processional
Welcome
Liturgy of the Word
Readings
Homily
Declaration of Consent and Intentions
Exchange of Vows
Ring Ceremony
Pronouncement of Marriage
Closing Prayer
Recessional

December 11, 2010

ELLEN REYNOLDS & KEVIN LAFFERTY

Stowe Acres Inn - Stowe, Vermont

THE WEDDING PARTY

PARENTS OF THE BRIDE	PARENTS OF THE GROOM
Mary and Hank Reynolds	Eva Peterson
	John Lafferty

MAID OF HONOR	BEST MAN
Marion Adelaide Kassler	Raymond Peterson

BRIDESMAIDS	GROOMSMEN
Amy Pelligrini, Lisa Herron	Frank Skelly, Sammy Tell
Rosanne Cunningham	Aaron Windover

OFFICIANT	READERS
The Reverend Michael S. Drake	Kelly Steillman
	Christina McPherson

▲ Sample of a wedding program

[126]

COMPOSING YOUR WEDDING PROGRAM

While formats for wedding programs vary, the information to be included is fairly standard.

The Cover

If your program has a cover, it should list the full names of the couple and the wedding date. Many programs also include the location of the wedding as well as a design element, often the same or similar element used on the invitation.

If your program does not have a cover, your program should begin with this same information.

The Order of Events

Your program should include specific chronological details about your service. This includes but is certainly not limited to:

> the name of the processional music and composer,
> the title of any reading, its author, as well as the name of the individual doing the reading,
> the name of any prayers,
> any specials rites or passages,
> the exchange of vows,
> the name of the recessional music and composer.

Many couples also choose to highlight lyrics from the musical selections or lines from the readings that hold special meaning to them.

You may also wish to explain any traditions, customs, or rituals included in your ceremony that may be unfamiliar to your guests. Where appropriate, it's always nice to invite them to participate in any officiant-congregation dialogue.

Members of the Bridal Party

This simple list familiarizes your guests with all the individuals participating in your ceremony. The list typically includes:

- The officiant(s)
- Parents of the bride
- Stepparents of the bride, if appropriate
- Parents of the groom
- Stepparents of the groom, if appropriate
- Grandparents
- Maid of Honor
- Best Man
- Bridesmaids
- Groomsmen
- Readers
- Musicians

Many people often choose to include a one-line note explaining the individual's relationship to the couple, such as "Sister to the Bride" or "Lifelong friend of the Groom." Their hometown or state may also be included.

Other Items to Include in the Wedding Program

Quite often a couple may choose to express their gratitude to their parents in the program with a thank-you note at the end of the program. A thank you to the guests is also considered appropriate.

If you wish, you may also recognize deceased loved ones in your program. Often flowers, candles, and candlelighting ceremonies are dedicated to specific individuals. It's also considered appropriate to include poems, quotes, and "loving thoughts" in honor of loved ones.

When are programs distributed?

Guests should receive a copy of the program as they arrive for the ceremony. Ushers may offer programs as they greet your guests or you may ask a family member or friend to assist with the task.

Alternatively, programs can be placed on a table for guests to pick up themselves on the way in to the ceremony or in the pews or individual seats.

CHAPTER FIVE

At the Reception

$\mathcal{M}$any times, it is the little things that make a reception special. While the meal, the dancing, and the company are the most obvious contributors to a successful reception, menu cards, place cards, and table cards can also add elegance to your affair.

TABLE CARDS

Table cards and envelopes are efficient tools for directing your guests to their appointed seats. Placed in the entryway to the reception hall, the envelopes have your guests' names written on them. Inside the envelope, the card has the appropriate table number written on it. When it is time to be seated, the guests open the envelope with their names on it and head to the table indicated on the card.

PLACE CARDS

When they arrive at their tables, your guests will notice place cards at each place setting. The place cards have just your guests' title and last name written on them. However, in situations where there is more than

UPDATED: *The Duogram*

The increased popularity of civil unions, hyphenated last names, and brides choosing to keep their maiden names, has spawned the creation of a new type of monogram: the duogram. Many couples prefer a duogram to a monogram as it respects the individuality of each member of the couple while presenting them as a whole. Duograms are also used by couples with traditional married names wishing to present themselves as a couple on their stationery.

Like a monogram, a duogram can be used on place cards, table cards, menu cards, and favor cards. Some couples even choose to have it embossed on their guestbook. Using your duogram at the reception is a nice way to re-emphasize the significance of the union that has taken place. Its appearance on your thank-you notes later will provide a nice visual recall of the reception and all the joy surrounding your happy day.

There are multiple options for duograms:

FIRST NAME INITIALS:
Heather and Robert Taylor

LAST NAME INITIALS:
Heather Landsman and Robert Taylor

B·V | R·C

FIRST AND LAST NAME INITIALS:
Becky Vitas and Ross Coleman

one "Mrs. Smith" seated at a table, first names are added to avoid any possible confusion.

Place cards are small cards, usually in a stock, color, and style that matches the wedding set or the theme of the event. A small monogram or duogram may appear at the top of the place cards.

MENU CARDS

Your guests may also find menu cards at their place settings. As the name suggests, menu cards list the menu items being served. The menu is listed in the center of the card. If wine is being served, the wines are listed alongside their appropriate courses. As with place cards, a monogram or duogram may appear at the top of the cards. Menu cards are usually shared by two people but there is no reason not to have one for each guest.

Menu cards always match the place cards. For small receptions, they are often handwritten.

FAVOR CARDS

A favor card is an appropriate way to again express your gratitude to your guests for their participation in your union. Favor cards come in a variety of formats and are typically inscribed with a message along the lines of "Thank you for sharing our special day." While favor cards may stand alone, many couples personalize the cards and attach them to a small gift that reflects an aspect of their reception.

A Look Back: ESCORT CARDS

Rarely used today, escort cards were small cards that told a gentleman which lady he was expected to escort into the reception. The gentleman's name was written on the envelope and the lady's name appeared on the enclosed card.

Sometimes a couple chooses not to purchase favors for their guests and instead use the money to make a donation to a given cause. That donation should be acknowledged through a small printed card positioned near each guest's place setting or in an attractive basket near the exit to be picked up on the way out. The wording on the card should note that, "In lieu of favors, a donation has been made to" a given organization. If the donation has been made in honor of an individual, it should also be noted.

CHAPTER SIX

After the Wedding

*W*ith all the attention that's paid to planning the wedding, it's easy to overlook the importance of post-wedding courtesies and essentials. But quite honestly, ordering your wedding announcements and your post-wedding stationery can be just as thrilling as picking out your invitation. The thank-you notes, folded notes, and gift acknowledgment cards you choose will be useful to you throughout your married life. You want to make sure that how you handle the presentation of your collective names through a duogram (see page 132), or other type treatment, represents who you are. You'll also want to make sure that it is something you'll be comfortable sending to loved ones and other members of the community that you may have need to thank or acknowledge in the future.

Ideally, your wedding announcements, thank-you notes, folded notes, and gift acknowledgment cards should be ordered at the same time you select your wedding ensemble. This will ensure a consistent look and feel to all the elements as well as give you no excuse not to get started on those thank-you notes!

WEDDING ANNOUNCEMENTS

Weddings are traditionally announced by the bride's parents, who may send announcements to relatives and friends not sent invitations to the wedding. They are sent after the wedding has taken place, never before. When circumstances permit, announcements are sent the day after the wedding. If the newlyweds eloped or the decision to send announcements was made late, the announcements may still be sent—any time up to one year afterwards is acceptable.

Wedding announcements follow the same format as the invitations. If wedding invitations are being sent, the announcements match the invitations. Many brides, however, send their announcements on stationery that is smaller than the stationery used for their invitations. There is no point of etiquette that suggests this as being more proper. Rather, it is a matter of personal preference. Like the invitations, wedding announcements are mailed in double envelopes. They are addressed using the same etiquette that is used for addressing wedding invitation envelopes.

The bride's parents "have the honour of announcing" the marriage. "Have the honour to announce" may also be used. A less formal phrase "announce the marriage of their daughter," is occasionally used, although its use may be misconstrued as suggesting the bride's parents disapprove of the marriage (since "honour" is not mentioned).

Since wedding announcements are sent after the wedding has taken place, they announce a past event. Therefore, the year is always included. It is written out on its own line following the date as "Two thousand nine." If the wedding was held in a church, temple, or synagogue, the name of the house of worship is mentioned beneath the year.

Wedding announcements may also be sent by the bride and groom themselves. The bride's name and title appear on the first line. "And" constitutes the second line. The groom's name appears on line three. The bride and groom simply announce their marriage. They do not "have the honour" of doing so since that would be presumptuous. Neither do they "joyfully" announce since their happiness is assumed.

Many couples include at-home cards with their announcements. At-home cards are small enclosure cards on which your address is given. (For more on at-home cards, see page 96.)

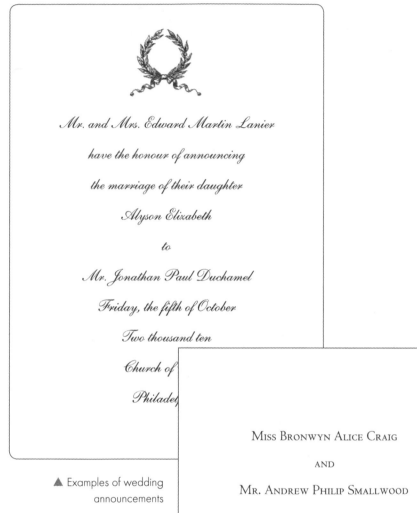

Mr. and Mrs. Edward Martin Lanier

have the honour of announcing

the marriage of their daughter

Alyson Elizabeth

to

Mr. Jonathan Paul Duchamel

Friday, the fifth of October

Two thousand ten

Church of

Philadel

▲ Examples of wedding
announcements

MISS BRONWYN ALICE CRAIG

AND

MR. ANDREW PHILIP SMALLWOOD

ANNOUNCE THEIR MARRIAGE

SATURDAY, THE SECOND OF JUNE

TWO THOUSAND SEVEN

CHURCH OF CHRIST

WILMINGTON, DELAWARE

We are having a small wedding. I would like to send announcements but I don't want anybody to think I'm asking for a gift.

Wedding announcements simply announce the fact that you have gotten married. They do not require their recipients to send gifts. Neither does the inclusion of an at-home card. At-home cards merely make it easier for your family and friends to stay in touch with you.

When should I order my wedding announcements?

Since wedding announcements are sent anytime from the day after the wedding until one year later, you have plenty of leeway in ordering your announcements. Most brides, however, order their announcements when they order their invitations. If you are not ordering wedding invitations, you should order your announcements as soon as you have all the pertinent information so they can be mailed as soon after your wedding as possible.

We are having a small wedding in August and a large reception in September. Is it proper to enclose a reception card with our announcements?

Invitations to a late reception should not be sent with your announcements. Your wedding and your late reception are separate events. They therefore require separate mailings.

THANK-YOU NOTES

Thank-you notes give you the opportunity to express your appreciation to those who were kind enough to send wedding presents. In addition to conveying your appreciation, thank-you notes also let the recipients know that the gifts they sent were received and not lost in transit. They should

ROOTED IN TRADITION: *The Most Formal of Thank Yous*
The most traditional of wedding thank-you notes are produced on ecru or white fold-over notes that match the wedding invitation. The bride's monogram is usually blind-embossed or engraved in a conservative color on the front of the note.

ROOTED IN TRADITION: *Registering for Thank-you Notes*
Thank-you notes are a wonderful gift and one that a family member or friend would be only too happy to give. Be sure to include them on your registry. You'll need to specify to the stationer you are working with and provide a "date desired" to ensure you'll have them to respond to any early gift-givers.

be sent as soon after the wedding as possible. Your thank-you note will seem more sincere if it is sent in a timely manner.

There's really no end to the number of choices you have in terms of style for your thank-you notes. Tradition dictates the use of a fold-over note with a monogram on the front and these are, of course, appropriate for all uses. However, you should feel free to select a note in a style that, while still formal, is a bit more reflective of your personality.

Sometimes it's best to have a few choices in your stationery wardrobe, using the most traditional notes for older relatives, members of the clergy, and others you are not that close to, and less traditional notes for extending thanks to bridesmaids and close friends.

Is it appropriate for me to send thank–you notes before my wedding?

You certainly may send thank-you notes before your wedding. Sending them as you receive the gifts is not only a courtesy to the people who sent them, it also cuts down the number you will need to send afterwards. However, remember at that point you still need to use stationery with your maiden-name monogram.

How should my monogram read?

The thank-you notes that you send after your wedding have the initials of your first name, maiden name, and married name on them. If all the initials in the monogram are the same size, your initials appear in order (first, maiden, married). When the monogram has a larger center initial, the center initial represents your married name. The initial on its left represents your first name while the initial on its right represents your maiden name (first, MARRIED, maiden).

Thank-you notes sent before the wedding should have your maiden-name monogram on them. Your first name, middle name, and maiden name appear in that order in monograms in which all of the letters are the same size. In monograms with a larger center initial, the center initial represents your last name. It is flanked on the left by the initial representing your first name and on the right by the initial representing your middle name.

On what page do I start writing my thank-you notes?

Monograms appear in the mid-center of the first page of most wedding thank-you notes. When that is the case, you begin and end your note on page three. On some thank-you notes, the monogram may appear at the top of the first page. If your monogram is at the top, you have the option of either starting on page one or page three. Your message should end on page three. (The whole point of using a small note is to limit the amount of verbiage you have to write.) If you do, however, have more to write, you would continue your message on page two. You should never write on the back of the note.

▲ Examples of monograms

My husband-to-be will be writing some of our thank-you notes. How should our monogram read?

Thank-you notes, like any other social correspondence, are personal messages written by one person. The thank-you notes that you write may be written on behalf of you and your husband but they are still written by you and you alone. Either your monogram or your shared duogram should appear on them.

If your husband-to-be will be writing his share of thank-you notes, he will be doing so on a thank-you note featuring a duogram or on his own stationery. Men use correspondence cards instead of fold-over notes for stationery. Correspondence cards are flat cards that are mailed in their own envelopes. Your fiancé's name or monogram appears at the top of the card. He should write only on the front of his correspondence card, a rule he will come to appreciate after writing his first couple of thank-you notes.

The name of the individual writing the note is the only name that should appear at the end of the note.

The separate stationery or duogram notes that you and your husband-to-be use for your wedding thank-you notes can be used afterwards for any other short correspondences.

I am getting married for the second time. What initials do I use on my thank-you notes?

Second-time brides use the initials representing their first name, maiden name, and new married name. The initial representing their first married name is not used.

I am getting married for the third time. What initials do I use?

Third-time brides use the initials representing their first name, maiden name, and new married name. The initials representing their first and second married names are not used.

I am keeping my maiden name. My husband-to-be will be writing some of the thank-you notes. How should the monogram read?

This increasingly popular dilemma is properly handled in a number of ways.

Your first option is to have each of you use your own stationery. Alternatively, you may also choose to use two small, separate, matching monograms—yours on the left, his on the right—joined by a small diamond.

The third and most contemporary option is the use of a duogram. The duogram blends your individual sets of initials (see page 132).

I am keeping my maiden name. What initials do I use?

Since your name is not changing, your monogram stays the same. You continue to use the initials of your first, middle, and last names.

Is it proper for me to use my middle name instead of my maiden name?

While some women continue to use their middle names after they are married, custom calls for you to use your maiden name as your middle name. By using your maiden name, you retain your identity as a member of the family into which you were born.

I am hyphenating my maiden and married names. How does my monogram read?

The initials you use represent your first name, middle name, and hyphenated maiden and married names. All four of your initials appear in order in monograms in which all of the initials are the same size. Your hyphenated maiden and married names appear in the center of monograms that normally have a larger middle initial. The initial representing your first name appears to the left while your middle initial appears to the right. The hyphen does appear between your maiden and married initials. Since most monogram styles are designed for three initials, you should request a proof to ensure that the monogram you chose looks good with four initials.

My new last name is McHenry. What initial do I use in my monogram?

You may use either *M* or *McH*. It is a matter of personal preference.

I would like to use single–initial notes for my prewedding thank–yous. Should I use my first or last initial?

Although there is no set rule, most women use the initial representing their last name on single-initial notes.

Is it proper to have our return address printed on the envelope flap?

Years ago, it was not considered proper for the return address to be engraved on the flaps of wedding thank-you envelopes. The address was either handwritten or left off entirely. Today, the postal service requests that all mail carry a return address so it is now appropriate to have the return address printed. It is also a great convenience.

How many thank-you notes should I order?

After you finish writing your thank-you notes, you may use your wedding notepaper for any short correspondence. Therefore, you should order enough to cover all your thank-yous plus extra for later on. It is a good idea to think ahead since stationery is less expensive per piece when ordered in larger quantities.

FOLDED NOTES

Folded notes are small, fold-over notes that are used for writing thank-yous. Traditionally, folded notes would have just the woman's full social name centered on the front. However, it is now common for folded notes to have the couple's name presented as "Mr. and Mrs." The inside of the card is blank for a personalized, handwritten note.

Can the engraving plate I use for my "Mrs." folded notes also be used for "Mr. and Mrs." folded notes?

Yes, since in most cases the "Mr. and" can be omitted. In fact, it is a good idea when ordering "Mrs." folded notes to order an engraving plate with "Mr. and Mrs." for future use.

I am keeping my maiden name. How should my folded notes read?

"Ms." is the widely used and accepted title for women who choose to keep their maiden name. "Ms." serves the same function for women that "Mr."

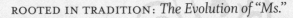

ROOTED IN TRADITION: *The Evolution of "Ms."*

It is a common misperception that the title "Ms." evolved from the women's movement. The term was first put forth by the *Bulletin of American Business Writing Association* in 1951 as a convenience to business letter writers.

does for men. It may be used with either the last name alone or with the full name. Like "Mr.," "Ms." does not denote marital status and may be properly used by both single and married women.

Is it proper for us to use our first names on folded notes?

Since folded notes are actually formal notes, the use of first names on them would create informal folded notes. If you would like to use first names on your notepaper, you should use less formal stationery such as a colorful note or correspondence card.

WRITING THANK-YOU NOTES

With the emergence of email for day-to-day correspondence, finding a personal note or letter waiting for us at the end of the day is always a pleasant surprise. Letters from friends and loved ones are special gifts. Someone has taken time from their busy schedule to share their personal thoughts with you. And, because of the permanence of a letter, it can be enjoyed over and over again.

If a letter is such a special gift, why do we write so few of them? In an age in which it is so convenient to pick up the telephone or to send an email, we see letter writing as a major event. We think that every letter or note must be a masterpiece.

Writing becomes a task because we feel that the quality of our letters must transcend the ordinary. Yet, when we receive a letter, we appreciate what was written and the thought that went into it, not how well it was written.

There are a few simple hints to follow to help you write your thank-you notes. Most of them simply require you to be yourself. Remember, the people to whom you are writing want to hear from you. They want to hear that you received your gifts and that you appreciate them immensely.

Don't Worry About Style

Write your thank-you notes in the style in which you usually speak. Use contractions; they're more personal. They'll make your notes sound more like you.

Don't Let Your Thank-you Obligations Pile Up

Write your thank-you notes the day you receive your presents. Your notes will be fresher and will sound more sincere.

Just Write

Writer's block comes from thinking too much about style and substance. You know pretty much what you want to say. Just say it. And don't worry about repeating yourself. Everybody understands that it's impossible to write something original on each and every thank-you note. Besides, your thank-you notes are not going to be passed around and compared.

Thank-you notes should be sent to everybody who sent you a gift or helped you with the wedding. If you ever wonder whether or not a situation calls for a thank-you note, stop wondering and send one. Whether necessary or not, it is always welcome.

Your thank-you notes should be handwritten and they may be brief. Since you write the thank-you notes yourself, you sign the notes with just your name. You may sign just your first name when writing to those closest to you and your first, maiden, and married names when writing to those who may need all three names to recognize you.

A tasteful thank-you note contains four basic parts:

1. A Greeting

   Dear Aunt Kelly and Uncle Steven,

2. A Note of Thanks

   The antique candlesticks that you gave us are beautiful. We really appreciate all the love that went into choosing them.

3. Mention of How Useful Their Gift Will Be

   A place of honor has been reserved for them on our dining room table.

4. A Suggestion to See Them Soon

   Nicholas and I plan on inviting you for dinner—and to admire our new candlesticks—as soon as we get settled in.

   Love, Jennifer

ROOTED IN TRADITION: *Acknowledging Kindness*

When writing your thank-you notes, be sure to think beyond the tangible gifts. As you plan and prepare for your wedding there will be many people who go out of their way to support you, assist in the planning, and host events in your honor. Be sure to extend a thank you to all of these individuals as well as to any wedding planners, officiants, stationers, and others who contributed to your ceremony.

GIFT-ACKNOWLEDGMENT CARDS

Back in the days when a honeymoon meant, for some, a cruise around the world or a summer in Europe, gift-acknowledgment cards were used to postpone the bride's obligation to send personal thank-you notes. Today, however, the reason is more likely an extraordinary number of gifts or pressing professional responsibilities. Nevertheless, gift-acknowledgment cards are still sent—sometimes even by the bride's mother—to buy the bride and groom additional time to send their thank-you notes.

Gift-acknowledgment cards do not take the place of thank-you notes. They merely acknowledge the fact that a gift has been received and mention that a personal thank-you note is forthcoming.

Mrs. Nicholas Jude Strickland

has received your very kind gift

and will write you later of her appreciation

CHAPTER SEVEN

For the New Couple

*S*teeped in the ultra-formal Victorian code of social etiquette, calling cards have made a fashionable resurgence in our fast-paced 21st-century lives. They are the perfect personal introduction for those occasions when a business card is too business-like.

For the new bride who has taken her husband's name, the calling card allows her to tastefully reintroduce herself to friends and colleagues, as well as to share her new address and other contact information.

INDIVIDUAL CALLING CARD ETIQUETTE

Today calling cards are also used as a convenient means of sharing contact information. These more casual cards do not necessarily follow the traditional guidelines regarding size and in fact can be produced in square, fold-over, and even die-cut formats. Cards often include an address, home phone number, cell phone number, or email address. Some people also choose to include a graphic or motif to convey a bit more personality.

If your calling cards are to be used as a gift enclosure, you may want to order matching envelopes.

A Look Back: THE HISTORY OF CALLING CARDS

Calling cards made their first appearance during the late 1600s. Small, decorative cards with hand-painted borders, they were engraved with the individuals' names and hereditary titles. Through the years, their appearance changed. The decorative borders gradually went out of style and by the 1800s, had disappeared completely.

Early calling cards were left by the European aristocracy when paying calls on fellow aristocrats. This practice eventually spread around the world. In the United States, it evolved into a very formal ritual with very stringent rules. Upper-crust women reserved one day a week to stay at home and receive calls. Other society ladies, knowing which day to call, stopped by and handed the butler their cards. After perusing the card, Madame decided whether or not she was receiving at that time. If she chose to receive your call, you were led to her drawing room where you chatted for a short period of time. You never stayed too long since she had other callers to receive. If she chose not to see you, you left your card and went on to your next call.

There were also rules concerning how many cards to leave and to whom they might be left. A woman could leave but one card as she was only permitted to call on another woman. A man, on the other hand, could leave up to three cards: one for the man of the house, one for the lady, and one for the couple. Turning down one of the corners of the card signified that it was intended for all the ladies of the house.

Although still practiced in military and diplomatic circles, "calling" is no longer practiced by the general population. However, calling cards still exist and are used for such diverse purposes as gift enclosures, informal invitations (although they are too small to mail), and to hand out to people one might meet in social situations, much as one would a business card in a business setting.

COUPLES CALLING CARDS

Whether united through marriage or a civil union, many couples opt for a calling card that represents them as a couple. These cards may feature a duogram highlighting both sets of initials, their names in full, or simply their first names and other contact information. No matter the style, the important thing is that both parties feel comfortable using the card as a part of their personal introduction.

Stacy+Jake

STACY ANDERS + JAKE KAMINSKY

313 STEADMAN AVENUE

MINNEAPOLIS, MINNESOTA 55444

612 555 1212

ANDERSKAMIN@AOL.COM

▲ Sample of couples calling card

MOVING CARDS

Moving, or change-of-address, cards are a nice way to inform family and friends of your new address and contact information. No formal rules apply to the format or design of moving announcements but it's always nice if they reflect your personality, the style of your new home, or even features of your community, such as palm trees. The wording of your card can be formal or whimsical but should always include your name(s), new address, phone, fax, and email address, if applicable.

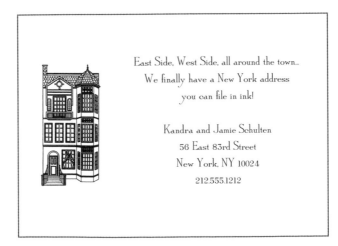

East Side, West Side, all around the town...
We finally have a New York address
you can file in ink!

Kandra and Jamie Schulten
56 East 83rd Street
New York, NY 10024
212.555.1212

▲ Sample of a moving card

PERSONALIZED STATIONERY

In our fast-paced and often impersonal world of digital technology—where messages disappear almost as soon as they are delivered—the arrival of a finely engraved invitation or a personal note on elegant, timeless stationery has greater impact than ever before.

Your stationery speaks volumes about you. It's your voice, your presence, when you can't be there to express your gratitude to a loved one or to share a special moment with a friend. When you assemble a stationery wardrobe, it will be helpful to keep in mind the impression you hope to make. Your stationery should reflect both your personality and the type of correspondence that you are sending.

Creating a stationery wardrobe requires asking yourself three important questions:

1. What kind of paper should I use?
2. What should I have printed on my stationery?
3. Should my stationery be printed or engraved?

What kind of paper should I use?

The same rules that applied to choosing the paper for your wedding invitation (page 27) apply to your social stationery. The finest paper is made from cotton. It has a rich, elegant feel that is always in good taste.

Stationery comes in many different colors. White and ecru, also known as buff, cream, and ivory, are the most popular but grey, blue, pink, yellow, and many other colors are also available.

You can order several different types of stationery. The two most basic are one for writing notes and one for writing longer letters. While these two items are essential, you may wish to add variations as you build your stationery wardrobe.

What should I have printed on my stationery?

How you personalize your stationery depends on the purpose for which the stationery will be used and on what is aesthetically pleasing to you. Your stationery may display your name, your name and address, just your address, your monogram, or even your husband's family crest.

Should my stationery be printed or engraved?

Like wedding invitations, stationery can be printed or engraved. The appeal of engraving lies in the exquisite detail created by its three-dimensional impression. Printed stationery is less expensive than engraved, and while it can be quite lovely, it does not provide the same quality feel.

SOCIAL PAPERS

There are a number of types of stationery that are appropriate to use for social correspondence. The type of paper used depends on the purpose of the correspondence.

Correspondence Sheets

Correspondence sheets are single sheets of stationery that fold in half to fit their envelopes. The sheets may be personalized with a monogram, duogram, name, address, or name and address. Many people often choose to include a motif that conveys a bit more about their personality or, perhaps, where they live.

Only the front of a correspondence sheet is written on, never the back. If you need additional space, use blank second sheets.

Monarch Sheets

Also known as "executive stationery," monarch sheets are used for longer personal letters and for personal business letters. Monarch sheets measure

7 ¼" × 10 ½" and fold into thirds to fit their envelopes. Monarch sheets are used by women but more frequently by men.

A name, address, monogram, motif, or name and address appear at the top of the sheet.

Only the front of the sheet is written on, never the back. If you need additional space, use blank second sheets.

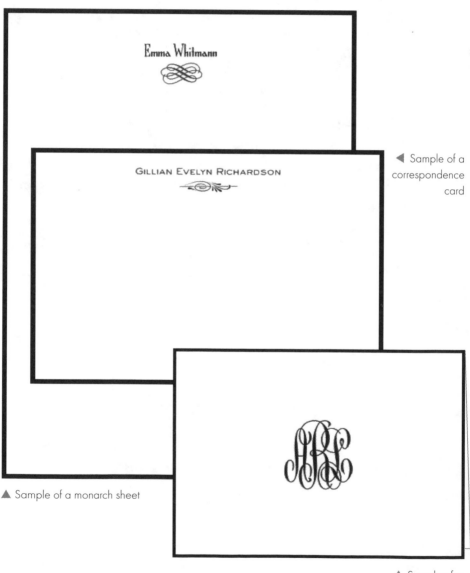

Emma Whitmann

GILLIAN EVELYN RICHARDSON

◀ Sample of a correspondence card

▲ Sample of a monarch sheet

▲ Sample of a folded note

Papers for Note Writing

Folded Notes

Folded notes are used to write thank-you notes, to extend informal invitations, and to send short messages to friends and acquaintances. Notes are customarily used as a woman's stationery, and can be personalized with a monogram, name, or name and motif.

In the past, folded notes were only available in ecru and white. Today, however, there is no end to the colors and motifs from which to choose. Even the envelope linings, frequently embellished with a motif or pattern, offer an opportunity to express your personality.

Correspondence Cards

One of the most useful items in a stationery wardrobe is the correspondence card. Used by both men and women, correspondence cards can be personalized with a name or small monogram. Less formal than a note, these increasingly popular items are used for thank-yous, informal invitations, and short notes. Only the front of a correspondence card is written on, never the back. If you need more space, use a different type of stationery, perhaps a correspondence sheet. (For more on correspondence sheets, see page 155.)

ROOTED IN TRADITION: *Letter Sheets*

Letter sheets are the most formal papers in a woman's stationery wardrobe. Letter sheets have a fold along the left-hand side and fold again from top to bottom to fit inside an envelope that is approximately half their size.

Blank, unadorned letter sheets are used to reply to formal invitations and for letters of condolence. Because of their simple elegance, letter sheets may be used for any type of correspondence. Letter sheets may be adorned with a monogram, duogram, a name, an address, or simply left blank.

House Stationery

House stationery may be properly used by any resident of your house or by any guest staying at your house. Many people keep house stationery at their country or beach homes so that stationery is always available for their guests and themselves.

House stationery typically features the name of the house or the address but can also be designed to fit the mood of the location. A graphic of a lake, a palm tree, or mountains are all nice ways to convey the feeling and spirit of the place.

ORDERING YOUR STATIONERY

Your stationery is an extension of your personal style. Today there are literally thousands of ways you can express yourself through paper, design, ink, and writing style.

Personalized stationery is best ordered from a respected stationer who has relationships with quality paper manufacturers and can offer you a complete range of styles and fonts. Many stationers will be able to create a digital image of your stationery at the time of ordering for you to approve or modify as you desire.

USING YOUR STATIONERY

In much the same way that there are guidelines for the wording and issuing of wedding invitations, there are also some basic rules surrounding the use of social stationery. Before ordering your stationery wardrobe you'll want to have a clear understanding of how and when different components are used. While your stationer should be able to offer some solid advice in this area you may also want to consult *Crane's Blue Book of Stationery* for guidance.

Even if you choose not to follow a reference and decide to set your own course for what papers to use and when, the best policy for any correspondence is to first write, and second, be sincere. A handwritten personal note conveys a level of connection and concern that is always welcome and appreciated.

Forms of Address

THIS APPENDIX IS INTENDED TO OFFER GUIDANCE on the handling of guests' names as they might appear on fill-in invitations and outside- and inside-envelopes for all types of wedding invitations. We have provided general guidelines to consider when preparing your invitations as well as some specific examples of how names and titles might most formally appear.

This information was prepared with the gracious assistance of Robert Hickey, Deputy Director, Protocol School of Washington®, Washington, DC.

Federal Officials

GENERAL GUIDELINES

HANDLING THE NAMES OF SPOUSES OR PARTNERS OF OFFICIALS:

For husbands use: Mr. (first name) + (last name)

Senator Helen Kinney and Mr. Robert Kinney

For women using their husband's last name use: Mrs. (last name)

Senator Robert Kinney and Mrs. Kinney

For women using a different last name use: Ms./Doctor/Miss (first name) + (last name)

Senator Robert Kinney and Ms. Helen Walters

For anyone using a different last name use: Mr./Ms./Doctor/Miss/etc. (first name) + (last name)

Senator Robert Kinney and Mr. Mark Henderson
Senator Helen Smith and Ms. Cynthia Parker

THE PRESIDENT OF THE UNITED STATES

	MAN	WOMAN
INVITATION	The President and Mrs. Smith	The President and Mr. Smith
OUTSIDE ENVELOPE	The President and Mrs. Smith	The President and Mr. James Smith
INSIDE ENVELOPE	The President and Mrs. Smith	The President and Mr. Smith

FORMER PRESIDENT OF THE UNITED STATES

	MAN	WOMAN
INVITATION	Mr. and Mrs. Smith	Mr. and Mrs. Smith
OUTSIDE ENVELOPE	The Honorable James Smith and Mrs. Smith	The Honorable Jane Smith and Mr. James Smith
INSIDE ENVELOPE	Mr. and Mrs. Smith	Mr. and Mrs. Smith

THE VICE PRESIDENT OF THE UNITED STATES

	MAN	WOMAN
INVITATION	The Vice President and Mrs. Smith	The Vice President and Mr. Smith
OUTSIDE ENVELOPE	The Vice President and Mrs. Smith	The Vice President and Mr. James Smith
INSIDE ENVELOPE	The Vice President and Mrs. Smith	The Vice President and Mr. Smith

MEMBER OF THE CABINET

	MAN	WOMAN
INVITATION	The Secretary of State and Mrs. Smith	The Secretary of State and Mr. Smith
OUTSIDE ENVELOPE	The Secretary of State and Mrs. Smith	The Secretary of State and Mr. James Smith
INSIDE ENVELOPE	The Secretary of State and Mrs. Smith	The Secretary of State and Ms. Smith

UNITED STATES SENATOR

	MAN	WOMAN
INVITATION	Senator Smith and Mrs. Smith	Senator Smith and Mr. Smith
OUTSIDE ENVELOPE	The Honorable James Smith and Mrs. Smith	The Honorable Jane Smith and Mr. James Smith
INSIDE ENVELOPE	Senator Smith and Mrs. Smith	Senator Smith and Mr. Smith

THE SPEAKER OF THE HOUSE

	MAN	WOMAN
INVITATION	The Speaker of the House and Mrs. Smith	The Speaker of the House and Mr. James Smith
OUTSIDE ENVELOPE	The Honorable The Speaker of the House and Mrs. Smith	The Honorable The Speaker of the House and Mr. James Smith
INSIDE ENVELOPE	The Speaker of the House and Mrs. Smith	The Speaker of the House and Mr. Smith

MEMBER OF THE HOUSE OF REPRESENTATIVES

	MAN	WOMAN
INVITATION	Mr. and Mrs. Smith	Mr. and Mrs. Smith
OUTSIDE ENVELOPE	The Honorable James Smith and Mrs. Smith	The Honorable Jane Smith and Mr. James Smith
INSIDE ENVELOPE	Mr. and Mrs. Smith	Mr. and Mrs. Smith

THE CHIEF JUSTICE OF THE SUPREME COURT

	MAN	WOMAN
INVITATION	The Chief Justice and Mrs. Smith	The Chief Justice and Mr. Smith
OUTSIDE ENVELOPE	The Chief Justice and Mrs. Smith	The Honorable Jane Smith and Mr. James Smith
INSIDE ENVELOPE	The Chief Justice and Mrs. Smith	The Chief Justice and Mr. Smith

ASSOCIATE JUSTICE OF THE SUPREME COURT

	MAN	WOMAN
INVITATION	Justice Smith and Mrs. Smith	Justice Smith and Mr. Smith
OUTSIDE ENVELOPE	Justice Smith and Mrs. Smith	Justice Smith and Mr. James Smith
INSIDE ENVELOPE	Justice and Mrs. Smith	Justice Smith and Mr. Smith

Diplomats

AMERICAN AMBASSADOR (AT POST, OUTSIDE THE WESTERN HEMISPHERE)

	MAN	WOMAN
INVITATION	The American Ambassador and Mrs. Smith	The American Ambassador and Mr. Smith
OUTSIDE ENVELOPE	The Honorable The American Ambassador and Mrs. Smith	The Honorable The American Ambassador and Mr. James Smith
INSIDE ENVELOPE	The American Ambassador and Mrs. Smith	The American Ambassador and Mr. Smith

AMERICAN AMBASSADOR (AT POST, IN THE WESTERN HEMISPHERE)

	MAN	WOMAN
INVITATION	The Ambassador of the United States of America and Mrs. Smith (for Man) The Ambassador of the United States of America and Mr. Smith (for Woman)	
OUTSIDE ENVELOPE	The Honorable The Ambassador of the United States of America and Mrs. Smith	The Honorable The Ambassador of the United States of America and Mr. James Smith
INSIDE ENVELOPE	The American Ambassador of the United States and Mrs. Smith	The American Ambassador of the United States and Mr. Smith

AMERICAN AMBASSADOR (AWAY FROM POST, OUTSIDE THE WESTERN HEMISPHERE)

	MAN	WOMAN
INVITATION	The Ambassador and Mrs. Smith	The Ambassador and Mr. Smith
OUTSIDE ENVELOPE	The Honorable The American Ambassador to Switzerland and Mrs. Smith	The Honorable The American Ambassador to Switzerland and Mr. James Smith
INSIDE ENVELOPE	The American Ambassador and Mrs. Smith	The American Ambassador and Mr. Smith

AMERICAN AMBASSADOR (AWAY FROM POST, IN THE WESTERN HEMISPHERE)

	MAN	WOMAN
INVITATION	The Ambassador of the United States of America and Mrs. Smith (for Man) The Ambassador of the United States of America and Mr. Smith (for Woman)	
OUTSIDE ENVELOPE	The Honorable The Ambassador of the United States of America to Chile and Mrs. Smith	The Honorable The Ambassador of the United States of America to Chile and Mr. James Smith
INSIDE ENVELOPE	The American Ambassador of the United States and Mrs. Smith	The American Ambassador of the United States and Mr. Smith

State & Municipal Officials

GOVERNOR

	MAN	WOMAN
INVITATION	The Governor of Iowa and Mrs. Smith	The Governor of Iowa and Mr. Smith
OUTSIDE ENVELOPE	The Honorable The Governor of Iowa and Mrs. Smith	The Honorable The Governor of Iowa and Mr. James Smith
INSIDE ENVELOPE	The Governor of Iowa and Mrs. Smith	The Governor of Iowa and Mr. Smith

STATE SENATOR OR REPRESENTATIVE

	MAN	WOMAN
INVITATION	Mr. and Mrs. Smith	Mr. and Mrs. Smith
OUTSIDE ENVELOPE	The Honorable James Smith and Mrs. Smith	The Honorable Jane Smith and Mr. James Smith
INSIDE ENVELOPE	Mr. and Mrs. Smith	Mr. and Mrs. Smith

MAYOR

	MAN	WOMAN
INVITATION	The Mayor of Dalton and Mrs. Smith	The Mayor of Dalton and Mr. Smith
OUTSIDE ENVELOPE	The Honorable James Smith and Mrs. Smith	The Honorable Jane Smith and Mr. James Smith
INSIDE ENVELOPE	The Mayor of Dalton and Mrs. Smith	The Mayor of Dalton and Mr. Smith

Religious Leaders

ROMAN CATHOLIC

	INVITATION	OUTSIDE ENVELOPE	INSIDE ENVELOPE
THE POPE	His Holiness, the Pope	His Holiness Pope Benedict XVI	His Holiness, the Pope
CARDINAL	Cardinal Smith	His Eminence Cardinal Smith	Cardinal Smith
ARCHBISHOP	Archbishop Smith	The Most Reverend James Smith	Archbishop Smith
BISHOP	Bishop Smith	The Most Reverend James Smith	Bishop Smith
ABBOT	Abbot Smith	The Right Reverend James Smith	Abbot Smith
MONSIGNOR	Monsignor Smith	The Reverend Monsignor James Smith	Monsignor Smith
PRIEST	Father Smith	The Reverend James Smith	Father Smith
BROTHER	Brother Smith	Brother James Smith	Brother James
MOTHER SUPERIOR USING FIRST AND FAMILY NAME	Mother Lesley	Mother Lesley Smith	Mother Lesley
MOTHER SUPERIOR USING CHOSEN RELIGIOUS NAME	Mother Mary Martha	Mother Mary Martha	Mother Mary Martha

	INVITATION	OUTSIDE ENVELOPE	INSIDE ENVELOPE
SISTER USING FIRST AND FAMILY NAME	Sister Lesley	Sister Lesley Smith	Sister Lesley
SISTER USING CHOSEN RELIGIOUS NAME	Sister Mary Martha	Sister Mary Martha	Sister Mary Martha

EPISCOPAL

	INVITATION	OUTSIDE ENVELOPE	INSIDE ENVELOPE
PRESIDING BISHOP	Bishop Smith and Mrs. Smith	The Most Reverend James Smith and Mrs. Smith	Bishop Smith and Mrs. Smith
BISHOP (MAN)	Bishop Smith and Mrs. Smith	The Right Reverend and Mrs. James Smith	Bishop Smith and Mrs. Smith
BISHOP (WOMAN)	Bishop Smith and Mr. Smith	The Right Reverend Jane Smith and Mr. James Smith	Bishop Smith and Mr. Smith
ARCHDEACON (MAN)	Archdeacon Smith and Mrs. Smith	The Venerable Archdeacon James Smith and Mrs. Smith	Archdeacon Smith and Mrs. Smith
ARCHDEACON (WOMAN)	Archdeacon Smith and Mr. Smith	The Venerable Jane Smith and Mr. James Smith	Archdeacon Smith and Mr. Smith
DEAN/MAN	Dean Smith and Mrs. Smith	The Very Reverend James Smith and Mrs. Smith	Dean Smith and Mrs. Smith
DEAN/WOMAN	Dean Smith and Mr. Smith	The Reverend Jane Smith and Mr. James Smith	Dean Smith and Mr. Smith
CANON (MAN)	Canon Smith and Mrs. Smith	The Reverend Canon James Smith and Mrs. James Smith	Canon Smith and Mrs. Smith
CANON (WOMAN)	Canon Smith and Mr. Smith	The Reverend Canon Jane Smith and Mr. James Smith	Canon Smith and Mr. Smith

PROTESTANT CHURCHES

NOTE: While Reverend is commonly used as an honorific in the manner of *Mr./Ms./Mrs./Dr.*, such use is not the correct traditional form. *Reverend* is a courtesy title and as such it describes an individual: This person is reverend.

Reverend is not traditionally used alone, with only a first or last name, or with a hierarchical title.

Correct traditional use would be: *The Reverend Craig M. Phillips, pastor of St. Ann's Episcopal Church*. So by tradition, "Rev.," "Rev. Craig," "Rev. Phillips" would not be correct.

However, since personal preference is always taken into account, follow the preference of the bearer.

	INVITATION	OUTSIDE ENVELOPE	INSIDE ENVELOPE
MINISTER OR PASTOR/MAN WITHOUT A DOCTORATE	Pastor and Mrs. Smith	The Reverend James Smith and Mrs. Smith	Pastor and Mrs. Smith
MINISTER OR PASTOR/WOMAN WITHOUT A DOCTORATE	Pastor and Mr. Smith	The Reverend Jane Smith and Mr. James Smith	Pastor and Mr. Smith
MINISTER OR PASTOR/MAN WITH A DOCTORATE	Dr. and Mrs. Smith	The Reverend James Smith and Mrs. Smith	Dr. and Mrs. Smith
MINISTER OR PASTOR/WOMAN WITH A DOCTORATE	Dr. and Mr. James Smith	The Reverend Jane Smith and Mr. James Smith	Dr. and Mr. Smith

CHURCH OF JESUS CHRIST OF LATTER-DAY SAINTS

	INVITATION	OUTSIDE ENVELOPE	INSIDE ENVELOPE
BISHOP OF A WARD	Mr. and Mrs. Smith	Mr. and Mrs. James Smith	Mr. and Mrs. Smith

JEWISH

	INVITATION	OUTSIDE ENVELOPE	INSIDE ENVELOPE
RABBI/MAN	Rabbi and Mrs. Glass	Rabbi Neil Glass and Mrs. Glass	Rabbi and Mrs. Glass
RABBI/WOMAN	Rabbi and Mr. Glass	Rabbi Miriam Glass and Mr. Neil Glass	Rabbi and Mr. Glass
RABBIS WHO ARE DOCTORS	NOTE: Use of Rabbi usually supplants use of Dr., but sometimes in academia, or by personal preference, Rabbi Dr. is used.		
RABBI WITH DOCTORATE/ MAN	Rabbi Dr. and Mrs. Glass	Rabbi Dr. Neil Glass and Mrs. Glass	Rabbi Dr. and Mrs. Glass
RABBI WITH DOCTORATE/ WOMAN	Rabbi Dr. and Mr. Glass	Rabbi Dr. Miriam Glass and Mr. Neil Glass	Rabbi Dr. and Mr. Glass
CANTOR/ MAN	Cantor and Mrs. Glass	Cantor Neil Glass and Mrs. Glass	Cantor and Mrs. Glass
CANTOR/ WOMAN	Cantor and Mr. Glass	Cantor Miriam Glass and Mr. Neil Glass	Cantor and Mr. Glass

Index